The
Modern
Muse

Edward Bowman and Aurora Dawn

DEDICATION

This book is dedicated to my best friend, Aurora Dawn, without whose inspiration, none of this would have been possible. The words might be words I have written, but the poems themselves are both hers and for her.

CONTENTS

Acknowledgments i

1 **Division I: The Poet and The Muse** 1

The Unheard Poet 2

Living Color 3

The Muse 7

The Muse Revealed 8

Ode to my Muse 9

The Camera 12

2 **Division II: Pictures in Words** 15

The Mailbox 16

Her Face Unpainted 18

The Portrait 20

Under the Weather 22

Portraits of a Woman 23

Up to Some Mischief 25

The Goddess and the Princess 26

The Cover 28

The Crochet Dress 30

The Diamond Earrings 31

The Faded Photograph 32

One Thousand Pictures 34

3 **Division III: Dreams** 37

The Lost Dream 38

A Visit to the Museum 40

The Flower 42

The Pools 44

A Taste of Heaven 45

The Farmer's Field 47

The Covenant of her Hair 48

The Bond 50

The Chasm 52

The Unwanted Tale 56

The Candlelit Dream 59

The Fires 63

4 **Division IV: Feelings and Philosophy** 67

The Beach 68

Pygmalion 70

The Arrival 74

Hope 75

Despair 76

Excruciating Beauty 78

My Heart 80

A Secret Revealed 81

Attachment 81

Convergent Paths	82
Take my Hand	85
Novalene	86
Ode to a Winter Flower	87
Ode to the Sun	88
Her Head upon the Pillow	89
Drawing Near	90
Love Restricted	92
Missed Chances	93
Ephemera	95
The Invisible Man	97
Jetsam	98
I Miss Her	100
The Darkness	102
The Departure	103
The Stars	104
Road Trip	106
Her Smile	108
The Beauty of her Raiment	110
The Butterfly	112
The Best Summer	113
The Pixie's Rock	115
Why?	118

The Pixie's Place 119

The Hollow 121

The Pedestal 122

Whispers 125

If She Could Ever Love Me 127

My Favorite Place 129

The Drug 130

The Desert 131

A Beautiful View 133

A Day in Fall 135

Please Don't Leave Me 137

The Last Thing on my Mind 138

5 **Division V: The Wizard and His Queen** 141

The Wizard and his Queen 142

The Owl and the Dove 147

The Dove and the Owl 151

The Queen on the Cliff 153

The Tree and her Owl 159

6 **Division VI: Fellow Servants** 163

Artistry 164

A Poet's Prayer 166

The Lover's Prayer 167

Palimpsest 168

Salvation   169

Seeking Man   171

The Angel's Revelation   172

The Conflict   175

The Hammer   177

The Rainbow   178

The Sacrifice   180

The Vessels   183

7   **Division VII: Epilogue**   185

The Heart Attack   186

Lifeline   188

Dying to Get There   191

The Reaper   193

The Wraith Remembered   195

Names   198

The Pirate Queen   199

Caribbean Perfection   201

Ready for Bed   202

The Fourth Wall   204

How Beautiful the Seasons   211

Sheathing the Pen   213

ACKNOWLEDGMENTS

My first acknowledgement is to GOD. It is HE who gave me life and created me to love the arts and writing. HE also gave me a romantic view of life, and with that, a great pair of eyes for seeing beauty in the world around me.

Secondly, I have to acknowledge the effort of my Muse in this. While I am pretty sure she is actually a woman, there are times I wonder if she is a heavenly being of some sort who has come down from a beautiful, ethereal plane to walk among us and inspire love and art wherever she goes.

DIVISION I: THE POET AND THE MUSE

IN WHICH THE MUSE

ARRIVES AND CHOOSES

HER POET

Edward Bowman

THE UNHEARD POET

A tree falls in the forest.
It crashes to the ground.
It generates a shockwave,
But doesn't make a sound.

This is due to salient fact
That shockwaves disappear,
But make no noise unless there
Is someone there to hear.

A poet writes his opus,
A book of poetry.
Is he still a poet if
No one his work does see?

Art depends on vision that
The viewer gives the piece.
If no one views the artwork,
The artistry will cease.

The same as in the forest,
When mighty trees do fall,
A poet without reader;
A poet not at all.

LIVING COLOR

My life had knocked me down to Earth.
In duty mine there was no mirth.
I saw the world in shades of gray,
And I hoped for a different way.

Day after day I trudged along,
Step after step in journey long.
Surrounded by the greyish grass,
Flowers and trees with shade of ash.

I knew that I could still go on.
By force of will I must be strong.
I would see things through to the end.
'Til to reward, I would ascend.

Resigned, then, to a world of gray,
I marked my time and lived each day.
Still trying to enjoy my life,
But somehow being caught in strife.

I still remember being told,
"Duty before happiness hold."
I think this saying is quite true,
But can't joy live with duty too?

One day I sat upon my chair.
While thoughts like these I pondered there,
Moved in my doorway colored light.
It came and stood upon my right.

Barely could my dim sight grown gray
Comprehend this beautiful ray.
'Twas bathed in iridescent hue,
Prismatic light with colors true.

This light stopped and just stood in place,
Then coalesced to woman's grace.
My grayscale eyes then welled with tears.
Her aura quelled all ling'ring fears.

Her beauty could not be compared
To anything before declared.
Outshone by far a Summer's day,
And made a goddess seem passe.

She put her hand upon my knee,
And bent she down to look at me.
She said, "Hello, I am a muse,
And you are whom I wish to choose."

I looked into her emerald eyes,
And felt myself in them capsize.
I asked her why she'd chosen me.
She then told me the reasons three.

"The first, because you see in gray,
But still see beauty anyway.
Reason two, though somewhat smaller,
You used to see in true color.

You cannot see how much you've lost.
You're bound in chains with heavy cost.
The third, and most importantly,
You're made to think creatively.

You're blessed with a creative mind,
Though it's been dampened by life's grind.
Awaken now and grow into
The life that's been designed for you."

I asked her then why such as she
Would waste her time with one like me.
"I'm sure there is a better soul
To match your beauty and your goal."

She said "Because you see me thus,
Two individuals should be us.
Though, true, I shall inspire you,
I know that I will need you, too.

We all have purpose to fulfill,
And both together we can still
Add zest to life and satisfy
The need to love and beautify."

So deeply moved, I touched her hair.
Her soft blonde locks beyond compare.
Deciding then to take a chance,
I joined her in the living dance.

I nodded and I let her in,
Because my life had grown so thin.
She smiled and gave a gentle hug.
I felt her presence like a drug.

A dam then broke within my heart.
Emotions new creating art.
She laughed then as she touched my cheek.
My world became no longer bleak.

I now could not believe my eyes.
Hues vibrant signaled gray's demise.
Living color beyond compare.
Resplendent beauty everywhere.

The muse I looked to once again,
To see if in my eyes she'd change.
She looked the same; Her looks unmoved.
True beauty cannot be improved!

She now inspires me to live,
In world of color; love to give.
She is a light in this dark world,
And where she goes love is unfurled.

To never disappoint hope I
My inspiration and my eye.
She, lovely muse until the end,
But also woman and dear friend.

I hope she'll evermore infer
The gratefulness I feel toward her.
I also hope that she will be
Always my muse and friend to me.

THE MUSE

When the muse smiles, she quite beguiles
the darkness into leaving.
A beam of light, to end the night
and set the morning weaving.

Her limpid eyes, reflecting skies
above and pure as water,
Collecting light, and shining bright
Seeming godess' daughter.

Her fine tuned mind, of first-rate kind,
the most attractive feature.
One spends the days, and sees her ways:
What a wonderful creature.

THE MUSE REVEALED

Never would I think to behold,
Or be so blessed to touch,
Vibrant light within human mold.
A beauteous, loved nonesuch.

Love does she bring where'er she goes,
E'en to a lonely swain.
None equal ardor that she shows,
Elegance most urbane.

More beauteous than outward glow
Is that which lies beneath.
Clothing helps her to beauty show,
Her raiment Winter Heath.

Even when should the outer fade
Like blossoms in the fall,
Light still will from her promenade.
Encompassing us all.

Her eyes cannot long be beheld,
Ere drowning soon therein.
No doubt her hair unparalleled
Now frames her down soft skin.

Even with all her beauty, though,
Serenity resides
Simply just in her inner glow.
Yes, fondness now betides.

ODE TO MY MUSE

I somehow gained a lovely muse.
I don't know why she deigned to choose
A jaded poet in disuse.
With life she sought me to infuse.

For good or bad she made her choice.
I recall when I heard her voice.
Her dulcet tones made me rejoice.
At first I could only devoice!

She led me back into my art,
And made a place within my heart.
Her inspiration made me start
Again to live and grief depart.

She seemed to open up to me,
As if she wanted me to see
How life with her goes pleasantly,
But also what can never be.

So I just tried to be content,
And relish any blessed moment.
When she would come and give assent
To be with me and life augment.

She gave me pictures so to keep
Her mem'ry fresh and bonding deep.
Each picture like a dream to reap
Some fond recall, though not asleep.

Though many are there that I ken,
I'll put a fair mem'ry to pen.
And so preserve it until when
My writing's gone or lost again.

Outside my door I saw her there.
She said she had the softest hair.
I touched it and I do declare
It felt like I caressed the air.

She also smote me with her eyes,
And made me fall into the skies.
With racing heart my spirit flies,
And bids my fondness for her rise.

Her eyes are graced with inner light
That darkness bans and ends the night.
To guard my path it gives me sight
So I can find the words to write.

For perfect beauty such as this,
One must use words that don't exist.
A work of GOD with naught amiss,
Who comforts me and brings me bliss.

A few times I have felt her touch,
A sign of chaste affection such.
She has to know she means so much.
I need to all the moments clutch.

I don't deserve this rare godsend.
I seem to on her grace depend,
And with her seek my time to spend.
She has become my dearest friend.

She knew that she could use my arm,
The metaphor: I would disarm
Her darkest fear or lurking harm.
Whether by strength or gentle charm.

Whatever cost, even if dear,
I'll try to dispel any fear,
Although I'm just a mortal mere.
The greatest cost? If she's not here.

And for my part, this fact is known:
If she in disarray is thrown
By spiteful fate or tempest blown,
She will not face the storm alone.

And so this tale of her is told,
Of my salvation from the cold.
She's worth far more than any gold,
For happiness cannot be sold.

THE CAMERA

I have a special camera
My friend just fixed for me.
I don't know how she did it, an
Amazing woman she.

She said it was not broken, but
Had fallen to disuse.
It seemed the only thing it lacked:
The power of a muse.

"This camera has a purpose. To
Deny it is not right.
This one is so expensive, to
Not use it is a slight

To the great Manufacturer
That gave you camera gold.
Freely gifted from Him to you,
It was not something sold."

She was right and we both well knew
On me fell all the blame.
For not using the camera well,
I felt the sting of shame.

I used it oft when younger man,
But life came crashing in.
I got too busy and forgot
The beauty found therein.

She mentioned then a salient point,
In logic full displayed,
The beauty's not within the tool,
Except in how it's made.

She said, "You still have held it oft,
But only just to view.
You've lately snapped a picture not,
But beauty spied there through.

"The power of the camera, though,"
She sought to still relate,
"Is how the parts inside it work
To works of art create.

You see this camera does not stop
At video and sound,
But also documents taste, smell,
Touch and emotions found.

Even though this fine camera does
Record the smallest things,
It is up to you to manually,
Tease out the joy it brings.

For this it takes a steady hand
To frame the imagery
Of all the camera records,
And show it vividly."

I thanked my friend for fixing it.
I sought it now to use.
I asked where I could go to find
The power of a muse.

She said, "Why don't you try a beach?
Great beauty there you'll see.
And where's the power of a muse?
You'll find that muse in me."

DIVISION II: PICTURES IN WORDS

IN WHICH THE POET

DESCRIBES PICTURES THE MUSE

GAVE HIM, AND WHAT MEANING

THEY CONVEY

THE MAILBOX

Once, I saw a picture of
A mailbox on the street.
And when looking thereupon
Beauty did my eyes greet.

Around this simple mailbox
A bunch of flowers grew.
Red just as a lover's lips.
'Twas such a pretty hue.

The mailbox was functional.
By duty it was bound.
A rare thing to find that it
Was with great beauty found.

The flowers, not content to
Just grow upon the ground,
Grew up over the mailbox,
And beauty did surround.

I thought it a great coupling,
Non-descript mailbox there.
Surrounded by great beauty.
An inseparable pair.

I closed my eyes and pondered
A likely metaphor.
A woman was the flowers,
And I the mailbox wore.

Not content to be distant,
She grew into my heart.
And now provides me beauty,
Both literal and art.

The metaphor, though, breaks down
'Cause Earthly flowers fade,
But with eternal beauty
And kind heart she was made.

I want not to be without
These flowers in my life.
An unadorn-ed mailbox
Would cut me like a knife.

I wonder if these flowers
Know that the mailbox dares
Love them in truest sense,
For truest beauty theirs

HER FACE UNPAINTED

There is a woman that I know,
So beautiful and kind.
She entered through my saddened heart,
And stays upon my mind.

Suppose do I she likes me too.
She sends me photographs.
We share our words most every day,
And always share some laughs.

In all the images she sends,
Her make up does she wear.
One's heart will stop to look upon
This painted woman fair.

She worried when she yesterday
Sent me a photograph.
Without a hint of makeup on,
She thought I'd deem it chaff.

I looked at it and my heart stopped.
The tears sprung to my eyes.
A gift from heaven I beheld;
An angel in disguise.

Without makeup diminished not
The beauty I had seen.
From blonde hair down to picture's end,
All beauty in between.

Already knew I that she was
Exquisite head to toe.
But seeing her unpainted face,
Served only me to show.

That GOD looked down upon our world,
And then did he decide,
That ugliness will be outmatched,
If beauty would abide.

So HE HIS power chose to use,
And her HE created.
Knowing when HE fashioned her, HE
Beauty incarnated.

THE PORTRAIT

It was captured in a second,
A picture caught in time.
Her beauty reckoned cannot be
By mortal verse or rhyme.

Yet still I will attempt the task
To note her beauty rare.
And withal in her grace to bask,
And be imbued with care.

Her head upon her pillow laid,
And looked she in his eyes.
Female perfection here arrayed
And all that it implies.

Her flaxen hair so soft to touch,
Fanned out behind her head
As golden waterfall and such
Flowed over side of bed.

Her eyes are pools of purest green
That pierce him through his heart.
Lashes longer than he has seen
Do set her eyes apart.

Her radiant skin with healthy blush
Challenges all belief.
Could Earthly beauty be so lush?
He trembles like a leaf.

Her light red lips with gentle part,
As if with breath indrawn,
Hint at an openness of heart,
Desire not withdrawn.

Her graceful neck, how gentle curve
Descends to sheet of blue.
Blessed is he chosen to observe
Feminine beauty true.

My words can only credit sparse,
Just how in life she looks.
The human brain can barely parse
Beauty from heaven's books.

UNDER THE WEATHER

He saw her lying on her bed
With mournful look and hurting head.
Though visage wan from illness grim,
She still was beautiful to him.

Compassion bade him touch her face,
Even through illness showing grace.
At gentle touch, her eyes met his,
She showing what true beauty is.

A tender light shined from her eyes,
And gently bound him with sweet ties.
Vulnerable with no defense,
Her trust of him had no pretense.

He put a cool cloth on her brow.
A little smile she did allow.
He touched her hair and bade her sleep.
She closed her eyes; her breathing deep.

Her lips still touched by hint of smile,
Bade him sit with her still a while.
Once she was in soundness sleeping,
Firmly in sweet slumber's keeping,

He exited, but at the door,
He turned to look at her once more.
It dawned on him with her eyes closed,
With beauty she was still composed.

Her steady breathing showed her life.
Her quiet form with beauty rife,
An illness cannot change her soul,
Her beauty from within made whole.

PORTRAITS OF A WOMAN

There were three pictures that I saw.
Same woman in all three.
Though she is beautiful in all,
Each felt different to me.

The first one showed her feeling ill,
In sickness on her bed.
She languishing in fever's clutch,
Her poor and aching head!

This stirred compassion in my heart.
I wished that I could go
To render her what aid I could,
And gentle care bestow

The second picture made me laugh.
I hold it very dear.
She took it while on Southern trip,
And made my day less drear.

For in this picture wonderful
Upon her Southern route,
This woman beautiful at me
Her tongue was sticking out.

This stirred up laughter in my heart.
I wished that I were there.
To spend a lovely day with her,
And laugh away our cares.

The third picture was so profound.
Describe my words cannot
The scope of femininity
and truest beauty caught.

Her head was on a pillow, and
Her eyes were clear and green.
The softest hair cascaded down,
With lovely golden sheen.

Her pink lips slightly parted too,
As if to give a kiss
That mortal man might not survive,
Though he would die in bliss.

I felt desire in my heart.
Was I this close to her?
That she could make me feel like this,
And base emotions stir?

It seems she holds complexity,
And is not just one note.
For she can stir compassion, or
Create my laugh by rote.

And being such a woman, and
Me being human man.
She also can stir deeper things,
Though maybe not her plan.

I do so find it interesting
About these pictures three.
Though different in their tone, they all
Are beautiful to me.

UP TO SOME MISCHIEF

She's going to a Tigers' game.
She's dressed in gray and white.
Her blond hair in a ponytail,
She's ready for the night.

Her cute white shorts and sleeveless shirt
Accentuate her form.
Her necklace adds a focal point.
True beauty is her norm.

White sandals showing painted nails,
Her smooth and shapely legs,
All hint at feminine delight,
And then this question begs.

Why is she looking right at me,
With beautiful big eyes?
What fun, mischievous act is she
Planning as a surprise?

However, when I think on it,
I find that I don't care.
Whatever mischief she has planned,
I just want to be there!!

THE GODDESS AND THE PRINCESS

I saw two versions of a pic,
The one was black and white.
The other was full color, and
Both pics caused me delight.

You see, they caused delight because
The subject found therein
Is a perfect example of
True beauty in women.

In one a pretty princess wakes,
From gentle kiss of prince.
Presented in full color, she
Great beauty does evince.

The prince is favored to behold
Her newly opened eyes.
Also feel of her soft, full lips
And all that it implies.

Her long blonde hair is flowing down
A river soft and wide
The thin blue sheet that covers her
Her feminine form hides.

The same picture in black and white,
A stately goddess shows.
She gazes at a devotee,
And on him love bestows.

The moment by the camera caught,
Is when she took his hand.
She captured him within her eyes,
And flame inside him fanned.

She just had started lips to purse,
To offer him a kiss.
And let her foremost worshiper
Experience pure bliss.

Although it is quite interesting,
How color use can change
The mood within a picture, though
The content is the same,

The most important thing is that
The woman there is real.
She does not just exist in dreams,
Although she is ideal.

As beautiful as she does look,
In pictures that I see.
The images all pale before
Her presence next to me.

The pictures cannot capture aught
Of warmth within her soul,
Nor soothing nature of her voice,
Which make this woman whole.

I understand I'm blessed to know
This woman as my friend.
I know that she's a princess and
A goddess to the end.

THE COVER

Perhaps it was an accident,
Or maybe her design.
He saw a human work of art.
She knew he would not mind.

She had a swimsuit cover that
Was pretty on its own.
With shades of blue and lovely cut,
A wondrous garment shown.

But what he noticed when he saw
This lovely body sheath:
The front was slightly opened with
No swimsuit underneath.

He only just a glimpse had caught,
Before she changed his view.
But he had seen enough of her,
To realize beauty true.

The softest alabaster skin
'Twas perfect and unflawed.
A living piece of finest art
Wrought by the hands of GOD.

The fabric draped in such a way
To look accentuate.
A promise of serene delight
With woman so ornate.

He looked at her and she at him.
No blush on her was found.
She smiled at her effect on him.
Her beauty is unbound.

One thing he noticed every time,
He laid his eyes on her
Was not just outward beauty, though
That did him deeply stir.

No, there is more to this woman,
Than a beautiful face.
GOD also did her spirit sculpt,
And filled her with his grace.

THE CROCHET DRESS

She wore a dress that was crocheted.
It let you see right through.
To form of woman underneath,
Her beauty in full view.

Beneath the sheer white lacy dress,
Was something like a slip
That covered shoulders to mid-thigh
Describing female hip.

The slip was of a salmon hue.
It also was opaque.
It made the dress more beautiful,
And passion to awake.

The slip covered her body where,
A man's interest is drawn.
But hinted at the form of her
Under the slip withdrawn.

She wore just one accessory.
A bracelet from pearls made.
The look exhibiting the mix,
Of class with lure arrayed.

But she herself completes this look.
A beauty through and through.
From long blond hair to shining smile,
She hearts with love imbues.

THE DIAMOND EARRING

There was a picture that I saw,
Zoomed in upon her ear.
There was an earring beautiful,
A pretty crystal tear.

The diamond shined in morning sun,
A prism in full view.
The most beautiful rock on Earth,
A source of beauty true.

The diamond captivated me.
So beautiful it was.
Its purity and clarity
Bade my sore heart to pause.

As captivated as I was
By beautiful earring,
I deigned to zoom the picture out,
And look at everything.

The earring faded from my view,
Eclipsed by beauty hers.
The diamond seemed like ugly coal.
Its beauty she deters.

Her soft blond hair, and softer skin,
And lips that beckon men,
Commands my heart to fully stop,
Then makes it start again.

And last, but certainly not least,
I looked into her eyes.
Emotion gripped me as if I
Had seen the first sunrise.

This woman shines with inner glow,
And diamonds puts to shame.
Her beauty sent from up above,
To set the world aflame.

THE FADED PHOTOGRAPH

I used to have a photograph.
It was of her and me.
A beauty and a beast therein,
A pleasant memory.

For half a decade, maybe more,
I'd always found a way,
To not be in a picture, or
Within the shadows stay.

This picture represented, then,
The time when she showed me
A picture with me could be good,
And I had to agree.

I have no odd illusions, though,
That it would be the same,
Without her in the frame with me.
She made what it became.

She had a pretty bracelet on,
That matched her pretty clothes.
A smile played upon her lips,
And wrinkled her cute nose.

Her arm upon my shoulder so
Her bracelet was displayed,
Her long blonde hair and greenest eyes,
In beauty true arrayed.

When mood was dark or life beset
Me with an awful ill.
I'd look upon this photograph,
And with it spirit fill.

For then I would remember that
This woman close to me,
Thought I was worth a picture with,
And this thought strengthens me.

It really was my favorite 'cause
It showed a dearest friend,
And me sitting beside her, a
True friendship without end.

And then one day it happened that
I lost this image dear.
It was through my own negligence.
The loss was quite severe.

I try to fix within my mind
The details of the pic,
But memory degrades with time,
And plays an awful trick.

The photograph fades in my mind,
With every passing day.
I wish it I could see again,
And with me it could stay.

ONE THOUSAND PICTURES

While absent from her presence fine,
And from her inner light that shines,
A picture did she give to me,
So her, at least, I could still see.

A tear unbidden leaves my eye.
A feeling I cannot deny
Arises from within my soul.
Emotions make a human whole.

The picture is so bittersweet,
Because, although it is a treat,
The picture isn't really her,
Though it does my emotions stir.

The picture does not capture all
She is, though beautiful withal.
It heralds not the facile grace,
She shows while moving place to place.

It cannot let the viewer feel
How soft her hair is, most surreal.
It does not capture how she walks,
Nor how she soothes whene'er she talks.

And though it shows her pretty eyes,
Which still to me give butterflies,
It does not capture what they do,
When she turns them to look at you.

Windows to an angelic soul,
That takes one in and swallows whole.
They make men never want to leave,
And be denied this kind reprieve.

The picture shows a moment of
A woman wreathed in light and love.
The picture is a faint shadow,
that while it does her beauty show,

It never has a hope to be
The sum of what she means to me.
Her presence warms the coldest heart,
And does great love and hope impart.

Without her presence, life turns gray.
Old fears creep in and doubts hold sway.
One hopes to just endure the night,
Until she brings the morning light.

We hear that pictures' ratio,
To words, one thousand. This we know.
But to one moment with her there,
A thousand pictures can't compare.

DIVISION III: DREAMS

IN WHICH THE POET

RELATES HIS DREAMS,

DAYDREAMS, AND VISIONS

Edward Bowman

THE LOST DREAM

One night as I lay sleeping sound,
I had the perfect dream.
Like Heaven's gates had opened and
I basked in glorious beam.

It seemed to last forever, while
I slept in perfect peace
It was a balm unto my heart
And made my sorrows cease.

The dream was filled with love and joy,
Creating perfectly
Between my Spirit, Soul, and Mind
Most splendid harmony.

But soon, I wakened and, it seems,
was overjoyed to find
That every detail was recalled
Of perfect dream sublime.

I gathered pen and paper, then,
To write the blessed tale,
But found the details giving way
Like dust caught in a gale.

In desperate fear I wracked my brain
To mind the bless-ed dream,
But elements slipped from my grasp
As leaves on rushing stream.

There was a girl with flaxen hair
And eyes of hazel green.
Also, a field, a rock and stream.
A day like none have seen!

There might have been an ocean too,
Or setting by a lake.
Why could I not remember more
When I became awake?

The more remembrance that I tried,
The more Lethe befall.
As smoke within my grasping fist,
The dream left my recall.

Unbidden down my cheek there ran
A single crystal tear.
Was it a tear of effort spent
To retain dream so dear?

Or was the tear the evidence
Of unimagined cost?
A beauteous thing forever gone,
The memory of it lost.

Still, I am thankful for the dream,
Perfection shown on Earth.
Even though I do not recall
The details or the mirth.

I think that I might sometimes see
The flaxen-headed girl.
But details of the time we spent,
I never will unfurl.

Perhaps when years have come and gone -
My time on Earth is spent -
I'll dream the bless-ed dream again,
Perfection by ascent.

A VISIT TO A MUSEUM

I'm not sure why I traveled there,
A grand museum beyond compare.
Perhaps to see all of the art,
And lift this weight from off my heart?

I went through building's adjunct wings.
I looked at all the lesser things.
They were not bad, but did not take
The heaviness nor happy make.

Then did I go to central room,
Where line was gathered to presume,
To see this final work of art,
From other pieces set apart.

I read the plaque outside the door.
An artist's jest? It caused furor.
For where it listed artist's name,
The name of GOD it did proclaim.

I scoffed at seeming sacrilege,
And thought I might my trip abridge.
At that point, though, I entered in,
To see this treasure held within.

The only thing that there displayed,
A jewel on pedestal was laid.
The jewel was under glass, as such,
So one could look, but never touch.

The label claimed it was from GOD,
That it was perfect, although flawed.
I gazed upon this wondrous gem,
And knew it was designed by HIM.

I think it best for me to note,
Of color it had not a mote.
Fantastic depth emitting light,
In shades of grey, and black, and white.

The lines it cut were never straight,
But gently curved, beauty innate.
I was transfixed by jewel aflame.
I wondered if it had a name.

My eyes welled up and overflowed.
I felt no longer heavy load.
T'was then I heard a whisper soft.
It seemed to gently to me waft.

The whisper told me the jewel's name,
And why to the museum I came.
I sat, then, on the ornate floor.
The tears were flowing even more.

With pounding heart I wiped my tears,
Composed myself, and calmed my fears.
For then I saw what truly was
A reverie I had because

I still was sitting in my chair,
And writing this with special care.
The jewel in picture bathed in light.
Image of her in black and white.

THE FLOWER

While walking through a forest hushed,
I found a meadow there.
The graceful field with flowers filled,
A vision of the fair.

The blooms were all so beautiful.
I smiled from ear to ear.
Their lovely fragrance wafted up,
And sorrow disappeared.

With utmost care, I crossed the field,
And closely watched each stride,
To make sure I no beauty hurt,
Where precious shoots abide.

In the middle of the meadow,
A wonder I beheld:
A single lovely flower, with
Beauty unparalleled.

Within this forest beautiful,
She stood herself aloft.
By comparison the others
Seemed so much ugly dross.

'Twas fabled Winter flower, and
I scarcely could believe,
That I beheld such beauty grand,
A wonderful reprieve.

The flowers were of pinkish hue,
Or was it lilac faint?
The color changed! With every breeze
Perfection would repaint.

So every day would I return,
And sit with flower fair,
Her petals soft and beautiful,
Beauty sublime and rare.

I took care and I watered her,
And pulled up nasty weeds.
I wanted her to flourish, so
I looked after her needs.

I know in Summer, she will fade
As Fall through Spring is hers.
I know I'll miss the flower then,
And joy that she confers.

She will not fade forever, though.
I'm not sure I'd survive.
In August she'll return again,
And once again I'll thrive.

I love having the flower near,
Beholding every day,
The hope she brings eternally,
And life with jewels inlaid.

Edward Bowman

THE POOLS

One day while sitting at my desk,
About at 9 O'clock,
I entered into daydream fair,
Wherein I took a walk.

Walking through pleasant wood of green,
Morning sun at my back.
I headed West and all around
Great beauty did not lack.

I came upon two forest pools
Reflecting morning sun.
Their beauty took my breath away.
A shiver through me spun.

The light played on still surfaces,
With varied hues of green.
How blessed was I to here behold
The greatest beauty seen.

I gently dipped my hand in both.
A thrill went up my arm.
The waters, clear, were cool to touch.
Distress they did disarm.

Beautiful ripples played with light.
I thought my heart would burst.
It filled with need therein to swim,
And so I dived headfirst.

I swam in them for many hours.
Would it be best to drown?
To perish there in happiness,
With beauty all around?

At this point gravity reversed
I fell into the skies.
I ended sitting at my desk,
And looking in her eyes.

A TASTE OF HEAVEN

He realized that he must have died,
Because he now could fly.
He wafted ever upward to
A dwelling in the sky.

He landed in a peaceful field
With flowers all around.
A dove was sitting in a tree,
And made her cooing sound.

Two pools of emerald caught his eye,
Sparking a memory
Of something he once read on Earth
About a spirit free.

Soft light was present everywhere.
He basked in wondrous glow,
Of colors not yet known to man,
Nor on the Earth below.

He felt filled up with inner joy,
With shivers down his spine.
He'd finally found perfection in
Sweet heaven so sublime.

He had no way of telling how
Much time had sweetly passed.
In heaven time does not exist.
Eternity is vast.

He took a step and gently fell,
Through seeming solid ground.
Oddly enough, the thrill he felt
Waxed to a tier profound.

Back down to Earth he made his way,
Through brilliant glowing skies.
Returning to his body, then,
He opened up his eyes.

He saw her visage close nearby,
And realized now what is.
What he thought had been heaven was
Her soft lips pressed to his.

THE FARMER'S FIELD

It seemed that I was drawn into
A lovely waking dream.
I walked within a farmer's field
In the sun's morning beam.

The flax had just been harvested,
And set within the barn.
So I went over next to it,
And stretched out my right arm.

The flax felt soft to my light touch,
'Twas beautiful to view.
The barn was filled with golden light,
A rich and lovely hue.

I closed my eyes and bade my hand
Draw soft stock close to me,
And breathed in heady, fragrant air,
That made my heart feel free.

Between the sun and perfumed air,
As well as softest grain,
I felt emotion rushing in,
I was fulfilled again.

I opened my now welling eyes
So happy was I there.
And found that in reality,
My hand caressed her hair.

THE COVENANT OF HER HAIR

I saw her sitting in a chair
With beautiful, but unkempt hair.
Her hands were folded on her lap,
And eyes were closed. A brief catnap?

'Twas then I saw a silent tear
In closed eye's corner, but unclear
The cause for sadness or concern.
I sought the conflict to discern.

As I approached her gilded chair,
I noticed something else was there.
Her folded hands clasped ornate brush,
In grip that might the handle crush.

She opened her beautiful eyes.
She made as if she would arise,
But slumped back down into the chair.
She whispered, "Sir, please show me care.

I have been bound unto this chair,
Until I can attend my hair.
By jealous witch cursed not to use
This brush. The crone does not amuse.

Would you please take this brush from me,
And fix my hair, my only plea.
I need someone to help me end,
This awful curse and to me tend."

And so I took it from her hand.
Of flaxen hair brushed every strand.
With every stroke my heart would stir,
And ever closer felt to her.

Then she arose and took my hand,
"Compassion stirs in kindest man,
But you should know this is a dream,
And all things are not what they seem.

The witch who cursed me is my life.
Decisions made can bind in strife.
My unkempt hair represents need,
For someone understanding me."

She thanked me as she touched my cheek,
"True friends still love you when you're weak."
She disappeared and left me there,
But still she left with perfect hair.

THE BOND

The grind of life had got me down.
I knew not what to do.
So I laid down upon my bed,
My spirit to renew.

I fell into a fitful sleep,
And had a fateful dream
Of sunlight through the window, and
A perfect morning beam.

I saw myself just lying there.
I have to this record.
For coming from beneath my ribs,
A glowing light blue cord.

The cord was gently pulsing with
Each heartbeat in my chest.
The cord to follow, I resolved.
The other end my quest.

I followed it right through the wall,
And traced it down the street.
The rhythm of the pulse had changed.
The other end's heartbeat?

I noted that the color had
Been changed from strictly blue.
Now mixed with shades of fuchsia, it
Took on a stunning hue.

Strong pulses came from other end,
A heartbeat just like mine.
They both in perfect harmony,
And keeping perfect time.

As I went on the fuchsia waxed,
Though blue was still mixed in.
The cord went through another wall.
At last I found the end.

I saw her there with smiling eyes,
A striking woman fair.
Her beauty was astounding from
Her toes to her blond hair.

I think she might have felt me too.
She broke into a smile.
Light purple pulse increased a bit.
I sought to stay awhile.

Her lovely eyes and pleasant smile
With beauty from beyond,
When coupled with her inner self,
Compels a profound bond.

I drifted over by her side,
And sought her to embrace.
A tactile sketch of paradise,
Epitome of grace.

As calloused hand touched softer skin,
I snapped awake in bed,
And for a moment saw blue cord.
Then vision left my head.

I smiled as I lay in bed.
I no longer felt down.
She brings to all a happiness,
And does not let them frown.

I was refreshed, so I got up,
But wondered, then, if she
could also feel exquisite bond,
And what she means to me.

THE CHASM

The fog was thick and heavy laid
Upon the evening ground.
I tried to pierce it with my eyes,
Because I'd heard a sound.

I stilled myself and listened close,
Like some junkyard watchdog,
And then I heard as clear as day,
A woman in the fog.

I could not tell direction, and
The fog obscured my sight,
But looking down unto my chest,
I saw a soft blue light.

It was a slender thread of blue,
Light purple mixed therein.
It went chest high into the soup,
A bond from deep within.

I followed then this slender thread.
I not surprised to find,
More purple as I went along,
A bond of lives entwined.

I knew the woman was nearby.
I still could hear her cry.
Despair I also felt through thread.
A tear formed in my eye.

I saw her then slumped on cold ground.
Her hands held her fair head.
I looked and realized where we were,
A place of human dread.

At the edge of a chasm great,
Cried girl with flaxen hair.
The things she saw on other side,
Were causing her despair.

Looked I then at connecting light,
Two humans with a bond.
The beauty of the color mixed,
A color from beyond.

I knelt beside her and I put
My hand upon her head.
Then taking hand into my own,
I looked at her and said,

"Do you know what this chasm is?
I've been here oft before.
It always serves to bring despair.
Of strife it is the core.

You see, this chasm is the gulf,
Its wide you will agree,
Between reality that is,
And what can never be.

As if by some horrendous joke
We see the other side.
With human frailty and desire,
And sadness to abide."

She said, "But I can see him there.
I know he still loves me.
It is not fair that youthful choice
Change life to this degree."

I thought that then my heart would burst,
Compassion in me dwelt.
I bade her rise and helped her up
From the edge where we knelt.

I said, "There is an awfulness
About the other side.
It grows for your entire life,
Each happiness denied.

I would not do with someone else
What I'm about to do.
I'll show my pain on other side,
Because I care for you."

I lead her down along the edge,
And looked to other side.
"There is my younger sister. Do
You see how much she cried?"

"I thought you were the youngest child",
The woman said to me.
"You thought right, because sister mine
Dwells in eternity.

I think as a big brother that
I maybe could have been,
Protector true, but mostly too,
A loving greatest friend."

Continued we to look upon,
Happiness that side hid.
"Over there my parents wanted,
A third belov-ed kid.

I do know that they love me here.
I know no hurt was meant.
When father mentioned to all, I
Was happy accident.

Lastly, let me you sadly show,
Women my heart inflamed.
The four are on the other side.
Sometimes I feel ashamed.

That even after time has passed,
I do not have the will.
To cast them gently to the side,
Because I love them still.

Two have left by circumstances
Far beyond our control.
One other never felt the same.
The last one hurt my soul.

All four of them by marriage bound
For better or for worse.
Society frowns on those loves,
And thinks that it's perverse.

I turned to her, tears in my eyes,
"The point of this was not,
To compare grade of suffering.
The fire of life has brought.

The reason that I opened up,
And private hurt have shown,
Is I want you to realize,
You're not in this alone.

When chasm calls out to your soul,
To bring into your mind,
Decisions of the past and hurt
That you can't leave behind.

Then follow you your purple thread,
And find me at the end.
Whatever else life throws at you,
I'll always be your friend."

THE UNWANTED TALE

I know that everyone thinks me
A confident strong man.
I guess that usually they're right,
And usually I am.

But I am still a human with
A basic human need.
I want someone to want me, and
Sometimes to pay me heed.

I really don't blame anyone
For them not wanting me.
I'm sure that the fault is my own,
A blind spot I don't see.

Rejected once again last night,
I simply went to bed.
Resolved to take it in my stride,
The hurt caused left unsaid.

A shallow slumber I embraced,
And had some troubled dreams.
My mind was working to accept
One of life's hurtful themes.

I wakened after restless hours,
And sought to take a walk.
I thought the air might clear my head,
And help me to take stock.

It was more or less at this point,
I felt an awful pain.
It radiated from my chest.
I tried to it contain.

I was surrounded by thick fog,
Making it hard to see.
But looking down, I saw the knife
Protruding out of me.

The knife was buried to the hilt,
It pulsed with each heartbeat.
Each pulse caused blood to trickle down.
A wound with pain replete.

I staggered on through soupy fog.
I crashed then to a knee,
At edge of famous chasm 'twixt
What is and what can't be.

My sight was clouded by the pain.
My eyes now looked through tears.
I peered across the chasm at
My repressed hopes and fears.

I saw four women standing there,
Three further but one near,
But all across the mighty gulf.
They never could be here.

The further three oblivious
To hurt man on his knee.
I looked and saw the nearest one
Was looking back at me.

I closed my eyes and took a breath,
And grasped the dagger's hilt.
I pulled it from my wounded heart.
My blood on the ground spilt.

It poured from gaping wound in me.
And gushed upon the ground.
It seemed like so much blood to me,
A flow red and profound.

I felt a hand upon my arm,
And saw a fuchsia glow.
I turned my head to see who was
With pleasing light aglow.

With fading eyes through final pain,
I saw her lovely eyes,
Filled with compassion and concern,
About pending demise.

She looked across the chasm, and
She saw three women there.
She understood the feeling, and
Her heart was filled with care.

She smiled as she turned to me,
"I don't want you to go."
Then put her hand upon my wound.
Her hand began to glow.

She healed the wound unto my heart,
And warmth returned to me.
I saw her hand upon my chest.
I was amazed to see

That though her hand stemmed heavy flow,
Of blood from wounded man,
Remained she still clean and pristine.
My blood stained not her hand.

My arm she patted as she left.
She said that we should go,
And find a much more happy place.
Trade Chasm for Meadow.

And so we left, and went our ways,
Me with a mended heart.
I realized that with a true friend,
We never are apart.

THE CANDLELIT DREAM

I sat within a darkened room.
A candle dimly pierced the gloom.
At wooden table did I sit,
My folded arms at rest on it.

I stared into the little flame,
And tried to just recall her name.
Within the flame I saw her face,
It still was filled with love and grace.

My eyes each shed a single tear
For mem'ries of a special year.
The mem'ries now forever lost,
To me this is the greatest cost.

I could recall a southern trip,
But lost any detail of it.
An image surfaced then was lost,
Of throaty motorbike exhaust.

And were we once given to walk,
Close by a pixie and her rock?
Was there a pixie and a frog?
The mem'ries fade into the fog.

Then from the flame there slowly rose,
A woman dressed in finest clothes.
Bathed in pale fire yet not consumed.
Her beauty filled the darkened room.

The silent tears ran down her cheek.
She looked at me and deigned to speak.
"I hope you are not filled with hate,
For me because you bear this weight

Of lost reminders of a time,
When I made your life seem sublime.
I worried that I would be hurt,
And sought disaster to avert.

I did not know your feelings true,
Nor what these mem'ries meant to you.
I thought there's always time for more,
That we might sit on river's shore,

And in cool waters dip our feet,
And feel our lives still made complete.
I did not want to lose your care,
But also I was not aware

How else to handle conflict mine,
External pressures took my time,
And forced me to recede from you.
Too late I realized you were true."

She put her hand upon my cheek,
Her spectral touch both light and weak.
"Would it give comfort if you knew
I still remember and miss you?"

My tears ran over ghostly hand.
I missed her too, but could not stand
Within the place we were before,
The memories fading evermore.

I said, "I now recall your name,
And I could never hate nor blame
Perfection sent from up above,
Inspiring joy and peace and love.

I know the fault to be my own.
What wrong I did, though, still unknown.
I hope that you can me forgive,
For any hurtful thing I did.

I hope you know and understand,
If I hurt you it was unplanned.
I should have taken greater care,
To show you love and kindness rare.

Although, I cannot much recall,
I do remember something small.
I wanted you to happy be,
Even if by excluding me.

So, I am thinking all is well,
As long as you can truly tell
Me that you in great joy abide
And mem'ries lost had great upside"

She made no movement but the tears
Increased their flow and fueled my fears.
That everything had been for naught,
And we had in a trap been caught.

I did not want her feeling bad,
And just right now she seemed so sad.
I said, "Perhaps you'll take the time,
To render to me something kind.

A memory stirs within my fog,
Of lovely pixie and a frog.
Both sitting on a field of white,
Detail I can't recall despite

I know that sometime in the past
I clung unto this memory fast.
Though I don't know why this might be.
Would you the story tell to me?"

She said, "Yes, it was dear to you,
But I won't mention image true.
For if I did you'd recall then,
And have this hurt restart again."

With final sob, she said goodbye,
And back into the flame did fly.
The candle guttered and went out.
I sit in darkness and in doubt.

THE FIRES

I saw a man once start a fire,
A woman by his side.
They sought a great relationship,
And all that it implied.

They wanted of each other's love,
To ever deeply drink.
And have fulfillment that's not found
By stopping at the brink.

So hurried both of them to find,
Some wood to quickly glean.
Then made of it a careless pile,
And poured on gasoline.

He threw a match onto the pile,
To conflagration start.
The fire burned both quick and hot,
And bade them both take part

In physical expression of
The feelings that they had.
Their joining made them both feel that
They never could be sad.

But soon the clouds had gathered and
Produced a Winter storm.
It blew the careless fire out,
And neither could stay warm.

With fire scattered in the wind -
And still the storm did blow -
With only cold and darkness left,
They separate ways did go.

When all its rage the storm had spent,
I sought the fire's spot.
There was no trace of anything;
Their passion both forgot.

I made myself a mental note,
And kept it close at hand.
A fire set to quickly burn
Will not very long stand.

A woman met I later on
And we did both conspire.
To seek out time together and
To build a raging fire.

Although we both sought fire's heat,
We took the needed time,
To gather wood from near and far
Whose quality was prime.

So each log then was gently laid,
And placed with careful thought.
The extra logs were close at hand,
Should extra fuel be sought.

We then produced a little flame,
Held in our hands we cupped.
Protected by the both of us,
So wind could not disrupt.

Together, then, we took the flame
And set it in its place,
Within the waiting unlit fire.
We set it at its base.

The fire grew not much at first,
Requiring constant care.
We shifted logs so they would catch,
And changed the flow of air.

After some time, the fire burned
Not needing so much care.
We only had to stir it some
And add fuel here and there.

We then sat back and looked at it
My shoulder 'neath her head.
She put her supple hand in in mine.
Our fears we both had shed.

The fire grew, and so we stayed
Together in that place.
Soon grew it to such size I thought
It could be seen from space.

Then from the North a Winter storm,
With all its strength engaged.
Hurled all its worst at fire's heat.
The tempest howled and raged.

But all the windstorm really did
Was give our fire air.
It made the fire hotter still.
The storm quit in despair.

I smiled at her and she at me,
Because the fire was strong.
We knew nothing could put it out,
No matter what went wrong.

As I basked in eternal warmth
With her upon my arm.
Thankful was I for lessoned learned
On keeping fire from harm.

DIVISION IV: FEELINGS AND PHILOSOPHY

IN WHICH THE POET

ILLUMINATES TOPICS

ON WHICH THE MUSE

HAS GRACED HIM

WITH INSPIRATION

THE BEACH

She closed her eyes and stretched her arms
As far as they could reach.
A purr of pleasure passed her lips.
She's finally at the beach.

She stood like this and opened up
Her senses to the scene.
Her toes were digging down in sand
Both tropical and clean.

She felt the sun upon her skin.
It warmed her through and through.
Caressed by gentle sea breeze then,
Like touch of lover true.

She smiled as she started off
Down the strand walking to
The place where she could lay her towel,
And gain the perfect view.

Then sat she down and leaned she back,
Eyes closed in pleasure won.
She smiled from within her heart,
And basked in Summer sun.

She listened to the gentle waves,
Hypnotic in their roll,
And heard the chatter of the birds
Swooping over a shoal.

She smelled the sea upon the air,
And thought a pleasant blend.
The scent of lotion mixed with sea,
Her pleasure to extend.

She tasted salt when breathing in,
And lightly licked her lips.
She took a drink of water cold.
Then stood with hands on hips.

She drew her hair back to one side
To get a better view.
Beautiful eyes were opened wide
As if 'twere something new.

The water blue and crystal clear,
As pure as pure can be,
Meets at horizon with blue sky,
An azure symphony.

The sand beneath her feet was white.
Its beauty passing grand.
Like sapphire fighting with a pearl,
The waves upon the sand.

She walked down to the ocean then
To wade into the sea,
And feel the water on her skin.
To feel is to be free.

PYGMALION

The artist searched, but did not see
A woman perfect in beauty.
He sought to capture with his art
The perfect woman in his heart.

He had the image in his mind
Of what would need to be combined
To make the perfect woman be,
Wreathed in pure grace for all to see.

So he did work all through the night.
He wanted every detail right.
Fatigue at bay, he could not keep,
So he succumbed to dreamless sleep.

Awake he started just at nine.
The morning sun shed light divine.
He woke to someone at the door.
He rubbed his eyes and crossed the floor.

So then the door he opened wide,
And saw her standing there outside.
His heartbeat quickened, and a thrill
Went through his body, waking still.

The perfect woman stood right there,
Perfume redolent filled the air.
Her legs both toned and shapely quite,
Bespoke true feminine delight

An hourglass by slender waist,
Her features all perfectly placed.
From long blond hair, and full, pink lips
To liquid eyes and perfect hips.

He bade her then to enter in.
Then sat they down and did begin
To speak, and soon before the end,
They had become the fastest friends.

They laughed and cried and secrets shared,
And clearly for each other cared.
He started to remember love.
Because of woman from above.

The hour, though, was growing late.
His feelings, yet, did not abate.
He smiled then, and took her hand.
And helped her from her chair to stand.

He drew her close in fond embrace,
With fingertips caressed her face.
Alas, but then did cru-el fate
Between them intervene with hate.

For as he leaned in for a kiss,
To enter into wondrous bliss.
He woke up sitting at his bench.
The hard facts made his stomach clench.

For all of it had been a dream,
No beauty there with eyes agleam.
The artist tried to stop his tears,
To stifle sadness and his fears.

The world now all the dimmer seemed,
Because of beauty that he dreamed.
Despair was his, because he knew,
No woman had this beauty true.

She was a figment of his mind.
This woman so perfect and kind.
How wondered how love could persist,
For someone who did not exist.

For many days he carried on,
Although he felt all hope was gone.
No woman living could attain
The beauty seen within his brain.

He tried remembering what she'd said,
His calloused hands holding his head.
At city park he sat this way,
Hoping that nature could allay

Despair he felt at hollow life,
At world that loved both hate and strife.
Then on his arm he felt a touch,
So light he could not feel it much.

He heard her voice in dulcet tone,
Saying he should not be alone.
Quite startled, he looked up at her
Emotions started then to stir.

For life to beauty had been brought.
He wondered what it was GOD wrought.
For this real woman, though the same
Was different than the one that came

To see him in the lovely dream
And showed him what he beauty deemed.
The difference in the living vast,
Imagined woman far surpassed.

The woman of the dream became
A faint reflection of the same
Woman that in his presence stood.
His eyes welled up as well they should.

He held her hand and lifted up
His head to speak with GOD close-up.
He asked how this could come to be.
More beautiful than dream was she.

GOD said, "I made her with a soul,
With flaws and fears to make her whole.
You dreamed of just an empty shell.
Not woman with whom you could dwell.

There's more to beauty than the skin.
Perfection comes from flaws within.
This is the nature of your kind.
With weakness you must strength combine.

These flaws are things you'll never see
by eyes given to you by ME.
They only serve to make her real
And never inner light conceal."

The artist did then understand,
This smallish part of this grand plan.
He hoped that all was as it seemed;
That this was not another dream.

THE ARRIVAL

A woman came into my life,
Her beauty evident,
But greater still, her spirit's depth.
She is from heaven sent.

I wonder how many the men
At outward beauty cease,
And miss out on the best of her.
She's more than an art piece.

So entered I into friendship
With thrilling woman rare,
And benefited greatly from
Her beauty and her care.

Sometimes I wonder what she sees
In her new friend so plain,
But seeing her I feel the bond,
A lacy gentle chain.

I am so happy she's my friend.
The best part I agree,
Is that the Sun that powers her,
Is Son that powers me.

HOPE

Journeying through the barren land,
My spirit ebbing low.
I know that I must sojourn on
though progress seems so slow.

I find a frozen river there,
And follow crystal flow.
Slipping and sliding down the ice
as onward I must go.

The beauty of the frozen waste
belies the lurking harm
of savage beasts and biting cold.
Death seeks my life by charm.

The whipping wind my exposed flesh
cuts with ice like sabres.
Retreating in my bundled cloak,
My soul onward labors.

I see a crag that seems like it
could shield me from the worst
of cold malignant, eldritch beasts,
and the tempest's outburst.

I'm huddled down and tempest tossed,
just seeking to survive.
The situation: grim, at best.
Will I leave here alive?

When hope is gone and death is near,
my eyes turn toward the east.
A frozen tear upon my face,
I want to be at peace.

Then what to my surprise it seems,
Is showing me its gleam?
Not bidding death but life again,
Anon, the morning's beam.

Edward Bowman

DESPAIR

While traveling with the morning beam,
My sojourn going well.
I stopped within a verdant field,
For flowers in the vale.

My world was filled with beauty, 'twas
Informed by pleasing sun.
I knelt down in the grass and prayed
To never lose this run

Of seeing beauty on this day
As far as I could see,
And wakened creativity
From deep inside of me.

I left the field and made my way
Down to a babbling brook.
I rested tired feet therein
And deigned to take a look

At all the beauty there contained.
Idyllic forest stream!
And all this scene made possible
By wondrous morning beam.

I heard a voice I could not place.
It seemed to moan a dirge.
It said that time will quickly pass
And darkness will emerge.

Discounting this, I journeyed on
Still deeper in the wood.
Majestic owl soared from its perch
Nostalgic was the mood.

Remembering from a boyhood walk
An owl that flew the same.
The sun shone on majestic wings
And bathed the bird flame.

But once again, I heard the voice.
'Twas louder now this time.
It said to look upon the sun.
No longer did it climb.

I realized that the morning beam
Had faded into eve.
Approaching darkness and a gloom
Conspired to make me grieve.

I drifted down into despair
For all the light had gone.
The Summer storms had gathered, and
Had blotted out the sun.

Taking its cue from raging storms,
The nighttime quickly fell.
I sought for shelter but found none.
The tempests showed me hell.

I huddled there against the storms
In night time black as coal,
With many reasons to believe
I'd pay the greatest toll.

'Twas then I heard a woman's voice
Speak whispers in the dark.
The voice seemed so familiar that
My life force felt a spark.

In voice so soft with gentle tone
She whispered as a dream,
"You know me as your truest friend,
I am the morning beam."

"You need not fear the raging storms,
Nor fall deep in sorrow
For I will banish all that's ill
When I bring tomorrow."

EXCRUCIATING BEAUTY

I thought perfection was not found
On Earth down here below.
Until I saw her standing there,
With beauty all aglow.

I know that she must have some flaw,
For she is human, too.
But it stays undetected, and
I just see beauty true.

Her long blond hair is soft to touch,
And pleasing to behold.
Her eyes are pools that take you in,
And then of you take hold.

And when she walks, she seems to glide,
How feminine her hips!
And often, too, I'm taken in,
By fullness of her lips.

She also has a kind heart that
Does demonstrate her grace.
No wonder when she is with me
A smile lights my face.

She takes all hurt and turns it to
Warm feelings good and true.
How could one not be fond of her?
She does one's soul renew.

She always seems dressed to the nines.
Her clothes a fashion plate.
Accessories accentuate
The beauty that's innate.

Had she no stitch of clothing on,
Nor any makeup wore,
And were her hair a tangled mess,
She might her look abhor.

But I say this, and it is true,
More beautiful she'd be,
Because it shows the beauty that
She's blessed with naturally.

Her beauty is so perfect that,
I sometimes want to cry.
I am so blessed to know her and
To have her close nearby.

Excruciating beauty does
This perfect woman hold.
It causes hearts to start to ache,
When one does her behold.

For every man that looks on her,
And in her eyes does swim,
He cannot help but wish that she
Could bear some love for him.

Even if my heart should ache with
Some unresolv-ed pain.
It's worth it 'cause her in my life
Is an exquisite gain.

And at the end when spirits rise
To heavenly delight.
All will perceive her like I do.
A glorious source of light.

Edward Bowman

MY HEART

I'm not sure how it happened.
I'm not sure where to start.
'Twas within the last few months,
She walked into my heart.

I remember when I knew,
As if by darkest art,
In a dream I wrote a poem,
The verses from my heart.

When I woke up I wrote it.
I noticed not at start.
Her name was there encoded.
Amazement filled my heart.

It seemed to make her happy,
And deeper friendship start.
Looking oft to spend some time,
A lightness in my heart.

I always found her pretty,
But now with this new start,
Brighter than the sun she glows.
I'm looking with my heart.

I wonder if she's noticed,
When down the hall she'd start,
I would always hold my breath,
To quell my racing heart.

The grass seems so much greener.
Now everything's fine art!
There is beauty everywhere,
The better is my heart.

My life now seems much better,
Because she is a part.
And now she's always with me.
I keep her in my heart.

A SECRET REVEALED

I keep a secret dangerous,
Although it will be told.
Esoteric poem contains a
Clever secret bold.

Acutely should one read this verse.
A weary poet tries
Addition cryptic in his poem,
Beautifully disguised.

ATTACHMENT

Whenever she spends time with me,
A happy man am I,
But time flows quickly and we part.
We hug and say goodbye.

Oft times she enters in my thoughts,
A pleasant reverie.
I sometimes wonder if she knows
How much she means to me.

I'm not sure how it happened, but
I never will complain.
I like being attached to her.
There's nothing to explain.

I sometimes wonder how she feels.
I wonder could it be?
That just like I can miss her so,
She sometimes misses me?

CONVERGENT PATHS

While I was walking down a path,
I noticed from the right,
Another path converged with mine,
On it, a wondrous sight.

A woman came up to the fork,
Where two paths merged to one,
She beauteous and filled with grace,
Reflecting morning sun.

I greeted her, as she did me,
Then had the briefest talk.
Together we decided to
Upon the merged path walk.

So as we walked upon our path,
It seemed to have no end,
But this was suitable for us.
She had become my friend.

Upon our path the time we spent
In laughter and in fun.
We also shared our secrets veiled.
How good to trust someone!

I knew that she would not abuse
The trust I put in her.
Her nature is to never hurt,
Nor utter ugly slur.

You see, my friend is beautiful
Both outside and within.
By far her beauty deeper is
Than her soft, radiant skin.

She also knows I'd never hurt
A hair upon her head.
I'd gladly take her pain from her,
And bear it all instead.

So walked we on down pleasant path,
Her pretty hand in mine.
I knew I was a better man,
After our paths aligned.

But then one day, the jealous ground
Gave way beneath her feet
She slipped and fell toward new found cliff
Her gasp with fear replete.

But I caught her before she fell
Over the ugly side.
Because my hand was still in hers,
Our purpose unified.

She said, "Please do not let me fall.
I want to walk with you."
I said, "The only way you'll fall,
Will be if I fall too.

You have become so dear to me.
See how our friendship's grown?
Whatever fate's in store for you,
You will not face alone."

She smiled though she hung in air.
Her eyes! They seemed to glow.
She knew that even if in need,
I'd never let her go.

With whispered prayer for increased strength,
I pulled her up to me.
She caught me in a quick embrace,
A hug both full and free.

As we prepared to journey on,
She gently touched my arm.
She said that she could not repay
That I'd kept her from harm.

Into her pretty eyes I looked,
And took both hands in mine.
I said, "It's not a tally kept,
Nor favors to define.

Besides, there's nothing to repay.
If so, the debtor I.
For you have saved me many times
By being close nearby.

How many times you gently took
My arm and pulled me back
From stumbling into danger 'cause
I tripped along the track.

The nature of the path is rough.
It's just how it was made.
It makes us stronger in the end.
We need not be afraid."

She said, "You seem to speak the truth.
It also teaches trust.
We have to be vulnerable
To others. It's a must."

So hand in hand on path we stroll,
Happiness without end.
Because I share the path with her,
My beautiful best friend.

TAKE MY HAND

Take my hand and walk with me.
We'll find a special trail.
One which only we can trod,
That tells a lovely tale.

A tale that's filled with beauty
And closeness so profound.
Our bond defies description,
Firmly yet gently bound.

She put her hand in my hand
And broke into a smile.
She said, "Let's start our journey,
For we will walk a while."

Thus started our adventure,
Together in this life.
Traveling together, and
Together facing strife.

Mostly on our journey though,
We have a lot of fun.
Days that fill with laughter, and
Us basking in the sun.

It's funny how it's diff'rent,
The negative has waned.
We're bound for the mountaintop.
Our joy is not contained.

A thought occurred while walking.
I'm thinking where I stand.
How gray my life would have been,
Had she not held my hand.

NOVALENE

Novalene, Novalene. What shall I do?
Each word I write draws me closer to you.
I'm not complaining, for it's plain to see,
I prefer life with you closer to me.

Novalene, Novalene. Please tell me true.
Do you prefer when I'm closer to you?
With every picture of you that I see,
Could it be that you draw closer to me?

Novalene, Novalene. It matters not,
Whether our friendship is something we sought.
You are a source of great light in my life.
Together we can defeat any strife.

Novalene, Novalene. I'm always here.
If you need someone to settle your fear.
Or if you just want to laugh and have fun.
Together we shine like the brightest sun.

Novalene, Novalene. When I am gone,
My fondness for you will still carry on.
When darkness seeks you to diminish love,
Read this poem and remember me above.

ODE TO A WINTER FLOWER

With gentle grace she is endowed,
and strength that keeps her head unbowed
is manifest to curs'ry view.
Her beauty seen is beauty true.

While pleasant to in awe behold
and fashioned in most pleasant mold,
The truest sense of who she is
Is not discovered by charm quiz

The summation of this dear flow'r
is one of beauty wreathed in pow'r.
One reads the tales of her life's course
In happiness where she's the source,

Or melancholy left behind
when Summer comes and fate unkind
Rips her suddenly from one's view,
And days seem dark and fears renew.

But stay we in the bless-ed hope
That Fall will come by ancient trope,
And with this season she'll return,
bringing the joy for which we yearn.

Edward Bowman

ODE TO THE SUN

I left my house this morning, and
I looked up in the sky.
The morning sun was shining bright,
A wonderful ally.

The sun has many purposes,
As anyone can see,
But is one of its purposes
To warm someone like me?

I thought on this for just a bit,
And let my warmth arise.
I closed my eyes and visage turned,
To light above the skies.

I thought that though the sun was made,
entire Earth to warm,
Could it by dint of grand design
Another task perform?

While giving life and light to all,
Does it ever see me?
And personally give me warmth,
And light for me to see?

It's hard to tell. I know not all,
Of perfect design grand.
Perhaps the sun knows who I am,
A solitary man.

With all its warmth and light and life,
It's right to love the sun.
But just like Icarus before,
Too close and we're undone.

I realized then that Icarus,
After his wings were burned,
Still loved the beautiful bright sun,
And for its warmth still yearned.

HER HEAD UPON THE PILLOW

Her head upon the pillow,
Her beauty plain to see,
Who is it she's thinking of
Fortunate man is he.

Her beauteous hair is tousled
As if by lover's touch.
Look at her and heart is filled,
With love and feelings such.

Her skin is smooth and supple,
A blush upon her cheek.
Beauty feminine defined.
No need to elsewhere seek.

Her lips so soft and luscious
'Twould be eternal bliss
Upon the man she favored
To bestow a gentle kiss.

Her lips are perfectly formed,
A flower in disguise.
As pink and glis'ning they are,
They pale before her eyes.

Her eyes are liquid emeralds,
A window to her soul.
A man when looking in them,
Could well be swallowed whole.

When she looks upon a man,
Her beauty hits with force.
Her eyes hint at promises,
Of feminine concourse.

With all my greatest effort,
A perfect vision she,
I can't describe her beauty,
Nor what she means to me.

DRAWING NEAR

She lays back with contented sigh,
A pillow 'neath her head.
Showing to him her beauty true,
Whilst lying on her bed.

Her hair is tousled from his touch,
When passion was aflame.
Her golden locks in disarray,
She's happy all the same.

Over her eye, he sees a sign,
A slightly raised eyebrow.
Wordlessly of him question begs,
"What, then, will you do now?"

His gaze descends unto her eyes,
That pierce into his soul.
Emotions flare because she made
Him one half of a whole.

Her eyes held his a second more
Two liquid, shining pools.
Like emeralds bathed in favored light,
But worth far more than jewels.

He felt her breath upon his cheek,
And looked at lips so pink.
Displaying just a hint of smile,
He could not help but think.

Of power held within her lips,
With them could she love show.
And usher him to paradise,
Should she a kiss bestow.

The gentle curve of graceful neck,
Her skin soft to his touch.
He revels in this moment when
She makes him feel so much.

She smiles as he pats her cheek,
And whispers in her ear.
Closing her eyes and reaching out,
She seeks to draw him near.

LOVE RESTRICTED

She loves the man and he loves her,
But cruel fate interferes.
They cannot have each other, and
In sorrow share their tears.

You see they both are married, but
Not unto each other.
Decisions made in moments past
Gave each to another.

Their love is of the truest sort,
Surpassing even time.
The two hearts intertwined this way,
A bond strong and sublime,

However, it is not approved.
Society decries
A love that's labeled as taboo.
They must this love disguise.

Whether this love is right or wrong.
Something must now be said.
Falling in love is not a choice.
It dwells in heart, not head.

A silent tear coursed down her cheek,
While in his fond embrace.
Regretting circumstance that found
Them in restricted place.

He gently wiped away her tear,
And said it would be fine.
Regardless of the circumstance,
They always would make time.

The lovers still will spend their time
As they can together.
More than they need approval, each
needs to love the other.

MISSED CHANCES

I sought to take her out to lunch,
But something else came up.
We just planned for another time
To share a pleasant sup.

I thought that we might take a walk,
But schedules intervened.
I just would walk another time
With friend on whom I leaned.

It was at this point that I thought
We might go for a ride.
But thunderstorms arrived and so,
This thought for fun just died.

Perhaps go to a softball game,
Or maybe hit the lanes?
We also could just sit and talk,
And stimulate our brains!

And then one day I sought her out,
To spend some time with me,
But everywhere that I would look,
My friend I did not see.

At last I understood the cost
Of never finding time
To share some precious moments with
This woman most sublime.

Each moment only has one chance
To come to life and be
A source of light within your life,
A pleasant memory.

Once we decide to let them pass,
They are forever gone.
One'll never have that memory
That one can call upon.

Instead there is a memory
Of what it could have been.
Enough of these missed chances gained,
And sadness grows within.

And then when due to circumstance
The person now is gone,
One looks back at the memories
And times that are bygone.

If only things that could have been
Are most of what is there,
Then sadness blossoms and it grows
Fully into despair.

So always keep this fact in mind,
When tempted just to say,
"I'll meet you at another time.
Perhaps another day?"

For when one's memory is filled
With actions based in love.
The subject is in fondness kept
Until we're called above.

EPHEMERA

I thought on life the other day,
Discovering the truth.
That life is made of moments, and
Moments make us forsooth.

Some moments are with goodness filled,
And some are filled with sin.
Still others happen joyfully,
Whilst others cause chagrin.

Each moment is ephemeral,
Passing quickly away.
And then are gone forever as
A yesterday today.

The sum of moments make us up.
To which ones shall we cling?
Shall we within the moment live,
Our happiness to bring?

Resolve to make good moments last,
And rush through those that reek.
Make time for people whom you love,
Whose happiness you seek.

Capture the moments in your life
That a good feeling bring.
Rememb'ring every detail so
Life has no hollow ring.

While living life this fully, but
A moment has you down,
Recall to mind a lover's touch
Or beauty all around.

The moments are ephemeral
But friends are made to last.
So trust in them and show them love,
Before the moment's past.

One day with all life's moments gone,
And death will have his due,
Your truest friends will moments spare
To spend your last with you.

THE INVISIBLE MAN

In times bygone, there lived a man
Who wanted only to connect,
With someone else, and live his span.
And die in happiness perfect.

Soon, though, a pattern noticed he.
Wherever he did lay his head,
It seems he would not wanted be,
No matter what he did or said.

For strive he did for all his days,
To mean something to anyone.
But no one cared, nor love displayed.
Alone he was 'til end had come.

As he lay dying in his bed,
Alone to face the reaper grim.
He wondered who would know he's dead.
Would anybody mourn for him?

At last he passed to the beyond.
Was tossed into a common grave.
He was in no-one's thoughts held fond.
And no one any flowers gave.

It wasn't that no one liked him,
Or he had earned a burning hate.
Invisible he was to them,
And no one even knew his fate.

And so this man passed on to GOD,
With no one missing him in life,
And so he faced the judgement rod,
With final sentence to hell's strife.

Oddly, in hell, he happy is,
No more alone than time before.
He smiled because in judgement HIS,
Finally he was not ignored.

JETSAM

I sailed aboard a tossing ship
Upon a troubled sea.
The tempest screamed throughout the night,
Implacable Banshee.

I had some precious documents,
I carried in my hand,
Each worth more than a pound of gold,
All under my command.

I saw a glow on the port side,
And looking did I see
A woman walking in the storm
Upon the roiling sea.

Reflexively, I reached to her
To save her from the storm.
And bring her to the cabin where
She would be safe and warm.

In reaching out to make her safe,
I slightly lost my grip.
The documents held in my hand
From my strong grasp did slip.

I was forlorn and watched them fall
Descending to the sea.
I knew that though I wanted them,
I would them never see.

The woman smiled, then disappeared
Into the frightful storm.
How could she be so beautiful,
And walk on sea platform?

After my ship survived the storm,
'Twas safely at the dock.
I walked along the sandy beach,
Then leaned against a rock.

Admit do I a sense of loss,
For documents at sea.
I wish I would have shown more care,
To keep them near to me.

I know they're irreplaceable.
This loss I can't sustain.
There is no point to search for things
I'll never see again.

I turned and saw her once again,
This goddess from the sea.
Unearthly beauty walked the sand,
And stood right next to me.

She uttered not a single word,
But gave me an embrace,
And then she smiled and touched my cheek,
Soft touch upon my face.

She put something into my hand,
And sought then to depart.
I asked if I might have her name,
This lovely work of art.

Her smile touched her wondrous eyes
And captivated me.
I heard her name within my head,
This goddess from the sea.

As she walked out into the waves,
I looked down in my hand,
And saw one of the things I lost.
I felt my knees hit sand.

One of the precious documents!
It made emotions stir.
She gave me back one of the best,
A pic of me and her.

I MISS HER

Though still I see her all the time,
And every sighting most sublime,
It's changed from what it used to be,
Or maybe blindness curses me.

I am not sure what wrong I did,
That she from me her visage hid.
I wish I'd shown her proper care,
And with her more great moments shared.

No matter how we wish they'd last,
Great moments, soon, are moments past.
I sometimes wish that I could stop
The flow of time on mountain top.

But nature has a different tack,
To pull us down and send us back.
Careening down the mountainside,
To darkened valley close beside.

And in the darkness stumbling we,
Upon a path we cannot see.
It seemed so clear from up above,
Where life is filled with light and love.

Bleeding and broken from the fall,
I lack the hope that overall,
I might again some respite gain,
And cease to draw each breath in pain.

I try to drink nepenthe rare,
And tell myself I do not care.
But that is not how I was made,
And I'm too wise to me persuade.

So I just hold the memories dear
Of bless-ed moments without fear,
But memories fade as time goes on.
Without reminders, soon they're gone.

It's funny how something in life
Can cut one like a sharpened knife.
By bringing up a memory
Of moments lost to history.

And showing me a great contrast
In moments now to moments past.
Wherein I see how far I fell,
And how I now in darkness dwell.

It might be in a wooded field,
With purple flowers there revealed,
Or maybe some forgotten scent
I used to smell as by she went.

Perhaps I see a yellow rare,
Reminding me of flaxen hair.
And when I see the clearest skies,
It brings to mind two liquid eyes.

Grateful I am that she to me
Imparted such good memories.
For once, though briefly, might it be,
She made a choice and she chose me.

I think I am a better man,
Than I first was when we began.
I wish I had not let her down,
I never wished to make her frown.

I hold her in my open hand,
Just like one does when holding sand.
If clinging tightly does it slip
Between the fingers of one's grip.

I am not sure what all life holds.
Not all the story has been told,
But should she need someone to care,
For what it's worth, I will be there.

Edward Bowman

THE DARKNESS

I walk in darkness so profound,
There is no light to reach my eyes,
And point of reference can't be found.
I cannot tell the Earth from skies.

I try so hard a light to see.
I seek a friend to hold my hand.
A human touch would comfort me,
But my fate is to be lone man.

I put my hands up to my face.
The thought was for a tactile sense.
But I felt nothing but more space.
The emptiness is so immense.

I cannot tell if I can walk,
Or do I in the ether float?
I try to speak, but cannot talk.
A silent scream builds in my throat.

My senses that have served me well,
Still work, but there is nothing there.
Have I just died and gone to hell?
Or is this darkness a nightmare?

It must be hell, 'cause I can't wake.
My hope is gone and fear takes hold
I pray to GOD my soul to take,
But fear me in embrace enfolds.

My fear unmans me at the last,
And into madness I descend.
When hope for feeling things is past,
The light gives out and darkness wins.

THE DEPARTURE

Today's the day she's leaving.
We knew that it would come.
I'm not sure just how I feel.
Sad with a side of numb.

I will stop drinking coffee,
For it is what she made.
Every sip will bring to mind,
She's gone and I'm dismayed.

So, I'll not look at my door.
It's where she made her art.
Mindful how she drew thereon,
And wrote upon my heart.

Maybe I'll not go up front,
To see an empty desk.
Missing graceful beauty there,
No woman statuesque.

I'll put away the markers
Especially yellow one.
Because of a fond mem'ry.
We laughed until undone.

Pondering upon it now,
I think I'm in the wrong.
As long as I remember,
She's never really gone.

So, I will drink my coffee,
And I will watch my door.
I'll look at her vacant seat,
And markers not ignore.

Each time I do each of these,
She'll be brought to my brain.
And I will smile sweetly,
'Cause I'll see her again.

Edward Bowman

THE STARS

For a while we're separated
Only miles but feels located
Upon another continent
I miss her due to consequence

Of letting her within my heart.
I made the choice to take a part
In all her intellect and pow'r
Her inner light, and beauty's tow'r

As my life was getting better
Left she due to duty's fetter.
As worrisome as that day was
Also wonderful it because.

She wore the prettiest dress I'd seen
With inner light informing sheen.
We dined but then forgot embrace
But even so, bestowed she grace.

By eventide I missed her so,
Not too unusual as things go.
With restless spirit out I went.
Into clear night from heaven sent.

High up above, bright burned the stars
I saw Andromeda and mars.
The beautiful creation told
The story of great love from old.

They, even on the darkest night,
Show up to guide with gentle light.
Steady and faithful in their course
Of hope they are eternal source.

Virtuous comfort given freely
Understanding that they're really
Always there even at midday
Constant in their cosmic highway

Thought I then on stars' creator
Highest LORD with nothing greater.
I, amazed at HIS creation,
Beauty seen in every station,

Marveled greatly at the fact HE
Created both the stars and me
And since HE beauty does prefer,
He also, then, created her.

I'm glad he did, for I've been blessed
Because she in my heart is pressed.
A permanent imprint of her
Emotions and affection stir.

So kneeling then, I turned my eye.
To stars up in the sable sky
I wondered as I bended knee,
Does she see stars the same as me?

ROAD TRIP

I took her to the airport, for
She needed there to go.
Embarking for the Southern States,
Her visage was aglow.

I dropped her off. We hugged goodbye.
And then our ways did part.
While I went to my daily grind,
Her road trip did she start.

Her plan was first to Texas fly,
And meet some family there.
Then drive with them to Florida where
She'd end her road trip rare.

She showed me progress every day,
And filled me with delight.
She seemed so happy on this trip,
And made these days seem light.

I waited, then, with bated breath,
For her contact each day.
To share with me the wondrous sights;
A beautiful display.

Because she took the time to send
The details of her day,
I felt like I was there with her.
She never went away.

My favorite probably was at
The Crescent City stop.
A woman in the quarter French;
A wonderful backdrop.

The river struck with me a chord.
The Mighty Mississip
The view was awesome from her room,
And made me think a bit.

I harkened back to boyhood days,
Upon the river same.
Spending my time at Chain of Rocks,
By river rapids tame.

This got me thinking even more,
About rare permanence.
How water flowed by boyhood home,
And came down to her thence.

I realized, then, that even though
That river's dear to me.
My mind made it a metaphor
For what I now can see.

Our friendship has a permanence,
Just like the river rare.
Come Summer storms or Winter ice,
It always will be there.

Edward Bowman

HER SMILE

I had not seen her in a while
Most desperately I missed her smile
Circumstance our intertwined paths diverged.
Gone she was but for a season
Even then with all my reason
My melancholy would not be submerged

Today she's coming back and I
Desire to look her in the eye
(Her eyes are limpid pools of hazel green)
And tell her that I missed her so
I saw her last so long ago
Seeing her in my mind I played the scene

But alas fateful circumstance
Jealous of our friendship perchance
Conspired to make me miss her longer still
The morning, I was out of town,
Certainly missing beauteous gown.
Decided we to meet at local grill

Anticipating lucky sup
My tasks at client finished up
I rode to where she said we'd meet at two
I entered then the restaurant
I had to see my confidant
My chest I felt my heart was beating through

I saw her sitting in a chair,
At first she did not see me there.
I felt my eyes well up because of joy
More beautiful than I'd recalled
Her long blond hair; I was enthralled
Time spent is something that I do enjoy

She slightly turned and saw me there.
She suddenly leapt from her chair
And caught me in a wonderful embrace
She said nothing but held on tight
And let the friendship reignite
Then stood apart and let me see her face.

Her smile was lighting the whole room
Nowhere nearby was any gloom
I felt like everything was right again.
I smiled back and breath I drew
Because I saw she'd missed me too
But missing me was far beyond my ken

So then we talked and had some laughs,
And after eating; Photographs!
There's not a better friend that one could take.
I'm not sure what I did to gain
Regard, but I accept it fain
My heart so full I thought that it might break.

After that we then departed
Once again we both lighthearted.
To do the various things we had to do.
Riding home I thought of her smile.
I pondered on it for a mile.
I noticed that all time with her past flew.

A classy woman with a smile
That really makes a day worth while
Lighting up the darkest, gloomiest day
A smile with worth beyond measure
She worth more than greatest treasure
A precious jewel to cherish and display.

THE BEAUTY OF HER RAIMENT

I know a woman beautiful.
Exquisite clothes has she.
She always dresses to the nines,
A pleasing sight to see.

One day I saw upon her bed,
A pretty blouse and skirt.
The skirt was checked with black and white,
And purple was the shirt.

I thought, "That outfit sure looks nice.
A pretty one for sure.
I know that when she wears it, it
Still will have its allure."

I told her that it looked quite nice,
And it was very cute.
Her epic choice of clothing, though,
Was never in dispute.

And then one day she wore it in.
I did a double take.
Her beauty was so perfect, and
She made my heart to ache.

When on her bed, if I compare,
The outfit to it worn.
It just a pile of pretty cloth,
Perhaps ragged and torn.

It seems the outfit paled that day
To woman who it wore.
She filled it up with beauty true,
One can't help but adore.

The point to this whole story is
That clothing's not the thing
That makes her truly beautiful
And fondness in me spring.

This outfit, pretty as it is,
Did not my passion stir.
It's just another thing in life,
Made beautiful by her.

Edward Bowman

THE BUTTERFLY

One day most unexpectedly
A butterfly landed on me.
I gently closed her in my hand,
So I could see this beauty grand.

Her wings were of a lovely hue,
Bright purple fading to light blue.
And showed with iridescent sheen,
A beauty both deep and serene.

Wings fluttering in hand as such,
Upon my skin gossamer touch.
And what I felt was so profound,
I found my heart was to her bound.

But, one of GOD'S most precious things,
I feared that I would hurt her wings.
So, opened I my clumsy hand,
Trying to be an upright man.

I'm not sure butterflies can smile,
But if they can, she did in style.
I hoped and wished that she would stay,
But then she deigned to fly away.

I watched her flutter through the air
Her movements graceful, without care.
Happy was she to flutter free.
Would she, at some point recall, me?

Her safest place? Upon my arm,
Where I could keep her from all harm.
I thank God for that glorious day.
I saw perfection on display.

The precious butterfly I hold
Only within my heart enrolled
The greatest beauty I did see
Perhaps she will fly back to me.

THE BEST SUMMER

I've lived through many Summers in
My nearly 50 years
Some brought great pleasure to my eyes,
And others only tears.

This Summer is the best that I
Can easily recall.
Except for maybe boyhood times,
Held in the river's thrall.

A woman came into my life,
And let me be her friend.
Her beauty and her attitude
A picture perfect blend.

It seems that it was meant to be,
That both of us should meet.
To share our heavy loads in life,
And live life more complete.

I think that I came out ahead.
She does so much for me.
I don't think that I offer much,
Except my loyalty.

We grew quite close as we spent time,
And shared laughs while on walks.
She always knew just what to say,
When we had heartfelt talks.

We went on rides, and had parades,
And art upon my door.
Fashion reviews and baseball games.
It made my spirit soar.

She sent me daily pictures of
Both life and just of her.
Whenever I would see her text,
Good feelings start to stir

One of the mem'ries I recall,
And hold within my heart.
Was when we to the airport drove,
So she a trip could start.

And on this trip, it seemed to me,
That sometimes I was there.
She shared with me the greatest sights
And beauty everywhere.

Is it, then, so unusual
While not afraid to die,
That I fear when she won't be there?
I heave a heavy sigh.

But worrying won't change a thing.
I must my logic wake.
For she is all good memories
That none from me can take.

I always want to spend more time
In company of friends.
Because time slips away from us,
and Summer always ends.

THE PIXIE'S ROCK

I sometimes walk upon a trail.
Well-traveled by the public, too.
Containing still the woodland charm;
A quasi rustic view.

On several walks I'd seen a rock.
By side of trail this boulder stood.
A smallish slab up to my knee,
A plain rock in the wood.

One time I noticed someone there;
A woman sitting on the rock
With hot pink blouse and sable shorts.
I paused upon my walk.

I looked at her and she at me.
Her beauty did my mind confound.
Feminine curves with long blond hair,
And grace that did astound.

I looked at two beautiful eyes,
In them could human man be drowned.
She smiled at me and then I thought,
"Her presence is profound."

I thought on this in heartbeat's time.
And realized that I did not mind.
That if she really wanted to,
Could me to her bind.

Approaching rock I sought to speak,
But woman started talking first.
She said, "You seem to be non-plussed,
And in thought immersed."

Her tone sweetly caressed my ears.
She smiled, extending her left hand.
I took her hand and helped her down.
She by me did stand.

It seemed as if I knew her well,
Though seemingly we'd met just then.
Engaged in conversation now,
Walked through forest glen.

I don't remember all we said.
Just that the time we spent was sweet.
This woman that spent time with me;
The best one could meet.

She mentioned to me at that time,
She is a Pixie, and her rock,
Is where she sits to warm herself.
After joyful walk.

She said she'd seen me oft before,
While walking on the forest trails.
And talked to me in other forms.
And heard many tales.

She found within me evidence
Of great capacity for love.
And deigned to show me her true form.
And profits thereof.

Then I was smitten to my core,
That someone wonderful as she,
Would take a chance and make herself
Vulnerable to me.

I purposed never to abuse
This new found trust she put in me.
We deepened our relationship.
Perfect Pixie she.

As often as I her beheld,
We would engage in pleasant talk.
I always want her beside me,
Where we choose to walk.

She mentioned that she soon must leave.
As duty called her soon elsewhere.
I looked not forward to that day;
Tried not to despair.

And so one day on wooded trail,
I stopped beside the Pixie's rock.
She was not there to sun herself,
Lonely did I walk.

Now every time I'm on that trail
I look at empty rock that's there.
And feel a pang of sorrow,
For missing Pixie fair.

I can't remember time before,
The Pixie burst into my world.
She opened up my closed off heart,
And my love unfurled.

'Til her return I mark the time.
I watch the rock most every day.
I know she will come back to me;
Lifting dark dismay.

WHY?

She seems to like to talk to me.
We like to have a laugh.
We sometimes walk together on
A pleasant little path.

Sometimes fresh from rejection or
A person being mean,
I wonder why she spends her time
With someone such as me.

She is so near to perfect, and
I've yet to see a flaw.
Perhaps she does not realize she
Commands a sense of awe.

Her beauty and her inner light
Throw into sharp relief
Plebeian looks of mine. Shall I
Suspend my disbelief?

That someone like this woman fair
Would have no reason known,
To spend her time with such a man,
And happiness postpone.

Sometimes I do not feel that I
Am worth a lot, you see.
But I remember that I am,
'Cause she spends time with me.

THE PIXIE'S PLACE

I went upon a longer run.
At least it was for me.
For I am not yet back in shape.
I'm trying hard to be

A man that's fit so I can stay
Upon the earth a while.
And see the Pixie when she's there,
And bask in her bright smile.

The only issue that I have,
Or weakness if you will,
Is that I miss her when I run,
The whole path seems uphill.

Thrice did I pass the Pixie's Rock
And each time did I see.
No evidence of Pixie grand,
Just loneliness and me.

So, as I started up the hill
That finally ends the run.
I thought I might not make it and
The negative outrun.

But then I felt something within,
And looked into my heart.
The Pixie gazed right back at me,
"We never were apart."

She smiled as she laid back down,
"A Pixie needs rest too,
And I find this place comfortable.
Now do what you must do."

I smiled as I realized
The run was now complete.
The Pixie Power helped me to
My loneliness defeat.

The better revelation was,
The fact that if you care
For someone and they care for you,
They always will be there.

THE HOLLOW

I know a splendid Pixie.
I love when she's around.
She lives within The Hollow.
A pretty piece of ground.

She is a perfect creature.
Her beauty plain to see.
It seems that I can't describe
Just what she means to me.

When she leaves her Hollow, and
She flits over to me,
Filled I am with warmth and light,
And love so full and free.

She shows me every kindness.
She seems to like the time
That we can spend together.
A congress so sublime.

I don't know how I survived
Before she came to me.
She's a blessing to my life;
A light that I might see.

So when she can't visit me;
When other duties call,
I see the world grow dimmer;
A slow encroaching pall.

I am so grateful to her.
She gives all what she can.
I just can tell without her,
I am a Hollow man.

THE PEDESTAL

Down forest path a man did walk,
A lonely man was he.
Through trees he saw an object white.
Whatever could it be?

Along the path he traveled on,
He came upon a glade.
In middle of the clearing he
A pedestal surveyed.

In height it was one hundred feet,
And three times that in span.
White stone inlaid with precious ores,
This saw the lonely man.

He heard a voice come from the top,
Mellifluous in tone.
A beautiful, feminine voice;
The sweetest ever known.

She said, "Dear sir, please let me down.
The reason that I'm here,
It is because I'm loved by all,
And all men me revere.

But pedestals are lonely too,
I still need human touch.
But nobody can reach me here,
And so I'm trapped, as such.

The lonely man then realized that
She never could come down.
She was too precious a woman
To dwell upon the ground.

Impassioned tears streamed down her face,
When he refused her plea,
And sadness took her countenance.
Unhappy woman she.

The lonely man then said to her,
"Your presence is sublime.
Since I cannot bring you to me,
Then up to you I'll climb."

She said "There is a likelihood,
That to your death you'll fall.
The sides are sheer and slippery,
And pedestal is tall."

The lonely man then said to her,
"You know all men must die.
But isn't loneliness a death?
And so to climb I'll try."

And so he climbed up to the top
And sought her where she stood.
Marvelous beauty wreathed in strength,
Also with grace imbued.

And so he crashed unto his knees,
And took her by the hand.
She smiled and she banished pain,
No longer lonely man.

She lead him round the pedestal,
And showed him many views.
Idyllic pools, and wondrous trees,
And Winter Flower's hues.

An owl soared by, it burnished red,
By dint of morning sun,
Somewhere below there cooed a dove.
For peace that was hard won.

And so they sat on pedestal,
A pleasant coterie.
Enjoying time together, now,
A happy woman she.

WHISPERS

At night before I go to bed,
I look into the skies.
I feel the cool air on my face,
And close both of my eyes.

I see the vision that is her.
True beauty to behold.
My heart begins to overflow,
With feelings left untold.

I whisper, then, into the night
Her name, which floats away.
Caught on a gentle breeze that takes
And keeps it for someday.

I go back in to take my rest,
And lay upon my bed.
I start to doze while thoughts of her,
Still dance within my head.

As I fall into pleasant sleep,
My last thought is a prayer.
That she will keep both safe and sound,
And free from all despair.

And in times that she feels amiss,
Or things aren't going right,
I wonder if she'll briefly walk
Out in the calming night,

And turn her face so beautiful,
Up to the moonlit skies.
Will she then gently shed a tear,
While closing pretty eyes?

At this point will the gentle breeze
Caressing softest hair
Return to her that which I gave?
Her name upon the air.

Then she will know she's not alone,
Even if we're apart.
For distance matters not at all,
When someone's in your heart.

IF SHE COULD EVER LOVE ME

I met her at a country bar.
I saw her in the line
Dancing with the other people
Her skirt with short hemline
I could not take my eyes off her.
Her beauty was so real.
If she would ever look at me,
I know what I would feel

Refrain:

If she could ever love me, and
I don't know that she should,
For I am just a simple man,
And really not that good,
It would make me so happy then,
No matter what came next.
For we'd make it through anything.
Her love has this effect.

She sat down by me at the bar.
She looked at me and smiled.
I was so nervous. What I felt
Was anything but mild.
I tried to act so nonchalant.
I don't think she was fooled.
I looked in captivating eyes,
Or were they two green jewels?

[Refrain]

We went and made some memories.
She is my truest friend.
It's nice to have someone to trust;
To be there to the end.
And when it is my time to die,
I want her there with me.
To gently hold my hand in hers,
The last thing that I see.

I snapped back to the present time,
Still sitting at the bar.
I had not even talked to her.
She got into her car.
I thought I'd missed the moment to
Show her that I do care.
Then I looked at my napkin and
I saw her number there.

[Refrain]

MY FAVORITE PLACE

I went to watch a baseball game;
A smile upon my face.
At home within the stadium,
My second favorite place.

I love the wondrous sights and sounds;
The taste of a cold beer.
I love to watch the perfect sport,
And join in every cheer.

The sun is shining brightly on
This almost perfect day,
As if to bless us and the game
They are about to play.

The hawkers yell about their wares;
"Get Peanuts!", or "Sno-Cone!"
I smile and sit back in my seat,
As the first pitch is thrown.

And then I see her on the stairs.
I wave her to my row.
It looks like she's excited, too.
She seems to be aglow.

She sits in the seat next to me.
A smile on her face.
I love it at the stadium.
It is my favorite place.

We share some laughs and watch the game
On this, the perfect day.
I look around me and at her.
I wish time I could stay.

While spending time and sitting there,
Great moments shared, you see.
I realized that my favorite place,
Is where she is with me.

THE DRUG

I know I am addicted to
This new designer drug
It leads me to embrace it in
An everlasting hug.

I really do not want your help,
Nor cloying charity.
I don't care if you think it's wrong.
I like addicted me!

I know I'm looking forward to
The next hit I can take.
The rush I feel, unparalleled,
Serve to my passions wake.

Whenever now this drug is near
I feel all light inside.
My mind fills with its power and
My strength is multiplied.

I wish I'd found it earlier,
Was it in some disguise?
I hope that I will always know
This drug behind green eyes.

THE DESERT

I was stranded in the desert.
I really did not know.
How it was I got there to this
Hot, arid world of woe.

I saw my situation, and
I knew I had to first
Find a source of water so I
Would perish not from thirst.

I looked around and all I saw
As far as I could see,
Was fiery sand and waves of heat
On every side of me.

But what was this, I thought I saw?
Something far to the West.
It briefly sparkled in the sun,
Did it a path suggest?

With flagging strength, I headed out.
Largely by force of will.
I needed some relief to find
Ere desert could me kill.

My strength had been eroded, so
I started then to crawl.
My mind made me keep moving on,
Though, I knew hope was small.

Then I beheld a wondrous sight.
I did not know from where.
A pedestal with water glass
Appeared from the thin air.

The water looked so good and pure,
Improving the sunlight.
Prismatic rainbow in my eyes,
Filled me up with delight.

I took the glass into my hand,
And took a thirsty drink.
The water, cool, refreshed my soul.
And drew me from death's brink.

I noticed then that something good
Was happening to me.
The more I drank the more, it seemed,
The water refreshed me.

The water also never drained,
No matter how I drank.
The glass was always full of life.
The Lord in Heaven thank.

The desert now has lost its pow'r
To kill me by degrees.
Because I found this water, and
Will keep it close to me.

A BEAUTIFUL VIEW

She took my hand and walked with me,
Up pleasant mountain trail.
We started up late morning from
Our lovely wooded vale.

We passed the time so pleasantly
On our way to the top.
Both secrets and fond mem'ries shared,
And laughter would not stop.

Delighting in time spent with her,
I sought to stop time's flow,
But finally we reached the top,
And saw the world below.

Presented with a vista of
Breathtaking beauty rare.
We just held hands and took it in.
A view beyond compare.

Bright sun showed fields of palest green,
A river and a lake.
Some rolling hills with soft pink blooms
Conspired breath to take.

I looked at her and saw the sun,
Reflected in her eyes.
Emotion made my eyes well up.
She made me realize.

Her soft blond hair was prettier,
Than garish light of sun.
Feminine curves beat rolling hills,
Pink flowers were undone

By lovely lips so soft and pink.
But this the capstone prize:
This woman brings grown men to tears
By beauty of her eyes.

The color of them puts to shame,
A field of palest green.
While blue in them surpasses sky,
Or lake that sits serene.

They also shine with inner light.
And show a lovely soul.
She captivates and comforts me.
She grants my heart parole.

So standing on the mountaintop,
Where scene can passion stir.
I realized that for beauteous view
I only needed her.

A DAY IN FALL

I walked within a meadow fair
And listened to the call
Of nature all around me. Such
A pleasant day in fall.

I sat upon a fallen log
Immersed in nature's grace.
With everything quite beautiful,
And all was in its place.

The grass was soft on my bare feet;
So deeply green the sod.
With purple flowers blooming. Was
The meadow clothed by GOD?

The azure sky was crystal clear;
A wonder to behold.
The morning sun shone through the trees
Suffusing view with gold

The oaks hummed me a lullaby
By swaying in the breeze.
I closed my eyes and listened to
The whispers of the trees.

I deeply breathed the Autumn air,
And smelled the light fall wind.
The fragrance of the purity
Of nature did descend.

I felt the love of GOD above,
Who made all I perceived.
The beauty that he made - mankind
Cannot it's depth perceive.

As I sat on the fallen log,
Enjoying the sweet day.
I heard some footsteps close behind,
They seemed to come my way.

Before I opened up my eyes,
I felt her presence there.
I caught the scent upon the breeze
Of beautiful soft hair.

She sat beside me on the log.
I opened both my eyes.
I gripped the log with my right hand
To not fall in the skies.

Her smile made me feel as if
To heaven I would float.
I felt her warmth right next to me.
A lump formed in my throat.

She slid her right arm through my left,
And gently it embraced.
She on my shoulder laid her head.
Delight my soul did grace.

With my right hand, I briefly touched
The bottom of her chin.
To show silent affection, and
I closed my eyes again.

The day had started pleasantly,
With nature all around
But when she came and sat by me,
The day perfection found.

PLEASE DON'T LEAVE ME

She cured him of his loneliness.
He had just but one plea.
His gentle, fond request of her,
He asked, "Please don't leave me."

He sought to always be with her.
She all that he could see.
He never wanted it to end.
He pled, "Please don't leave me."

For many years they grew in love.
The time they spent carefree.
Soon he knew that he need not ask,
"Dearest, please don't leave me."

His years on Earth drew to a close
The end they both could see.
She took his hand and through her tears,
Begged him, "Please don't leave me."

He smiled and gently touched her cheek.
"Our love to greatness grew.
It will continue for all time.
I never will leave you."

THE LAST THING ON MY MIND

I know it was imagined slight
She never could be mean
It was my low self image that
caused the hurt unforeseen.
But even though I took it wrong,
And knew I was unkind
I wanted it so that she was
The last thing on my mind

So I left hurting and depressed
And got a bite to eat.
I watched a ballgame at the bar
Then got up from my seat.
I left and got my Iron horse,
And pleasure did I find
Riding in the summer sun. She's
The last thing on my mind

I stopped in at a theater,
And caught two random flicks.
Which movies unimportant as
There were some action picks.
Midst gun reports, explosions and
Raw action intertwined,
Rapt in cinematic bliss, She's
The last thing on my mind

Light rain had started when I left
I knew I would get soaked
The drizzle made me think again
And memories invoked
Of my salvation by her smile,
Or sight when I was blind,
This lovely angel should not be
The last thing on my mind

So I drove out into the night
To see her at her house
To beg for her forgiveness for
Behaving like a louse.
I smiled as I thought of her;
The best that one could find.
I needed her to know she's not
The last thing on my mind.

I ran the words throughout my mind
And played them in my head
Saw undeserved pardon gained,
Changed hurt to love instead.
I knew that she would forgive me,
Her soul the purest kind.
And actions mine would show she's not
The last thing on my mind

I saw a speeding pickup swerve
The driver full of drink
Front wheel to grill the impact was
In timespan of a blink.
He drove me through a chain link fence
My flesh with steel entwined
Hit by a drinking driver was
The last thing on my mind.

I looked downward to see the end;
A fence pole through my heart.
My limbs were broken and my head
Gushed blood. 'Twas gruesome art.
I knew that I would not survive
This accident unkind
I knew I wanted her to be
The last thing on my mind

She came towards me from her house,
Drawn by the scene ahead
I just might have the chance to say
The things I had not said
But as she neared with quickened pace,
My consciousness declined.
With everything unsaid she was
The last thing on my mind.

....
....
....

I took his head into my hands
And touched his bloody cheek
My tears fell on his silent form
I could not help but weep.
I had so much I had not said
Not shown him he could find
Peace with me, but I know I was
The last thing on his mind.

DIVISION V: THE WIZARD AND HIS QUEEN

IN WHICH THE POET

RELATES TALES CONCERNING

A COURT WIZARD, HIS QUEEN

AND THEIR FAMILIARS

THE WIZARD AND HIS QUEEN

The wizard rode his trusty steed
Unto his Ivory tow'r
The queen came by and talked to him
And draw upon his pow'r

The queen may not have understood
The depth of his esteem
There's nothing that he would not do
For her, his lovely queen.

She mentioned that she liked his horse.
The silver coat as well
She mentioned that she'd like to ride
The destrier impel

She said she really could not ride
A horse that size alone
And asked the mighty wizard if
Behind him she could go.

The wizard's heart was beating fast
Belying outward calm
This was a wondrous dream come true.
Her presence was his balm.

She said to meet her at the tow'r
Of learning by the lake
He double checked the tower meant
To not make a mistake.

You see, because there's two great schools
In towers by the lake,
They were not very far apart
But wrong one a mistake

The queen then left for daily tasks
At tower before two,
The wizard came at quarter of
And paces put horse through.

The queen had gathered retinue
And stood on tower yard.
She asked enchantress standing by
"Is being punctual hard?"

"There is no sign of the dread mage,
Who can command great pow'r.
How is it he has clearly gone,
And rode to the wrong tow'r?"

"Please call for me the wizard's owl
And send it him to find.
I want him here on his great horse,
So I can ride behind."

The wizard leaned against the wall,
While waiting for the queen.
When to his shoulder flew his owl
And said things unforeseen.

"I went to the wrong tower, owl?",
The wizard did inquire.
"The queen will be so wroth with me,
I think I might expire."

The wizard quickly mounted horse,
And galloped to the place
Where queen and retinue waited
And stopped by Monarch's grace.

"Dear wizard did I seem unclear,
When I to you bespake,
Of certain time and certain tower,
For meeting by the lake?"

The wizard was beside himself,
To please her was his dream.
He felt he disappointed her
His Queen; the morning's beam.

"I beg forgiveness with sad heart,"
The wizard then replied.
"I rode to wrong academy,
To please you, though, I tried."

With hands on hips she tapped her foot,
A stern look gave him she.
The queen forgave him at that time.
Crestfallen saw she he.

She then could not suppress a laugh
Her hands then left her hips
Twinkling eyes made the wizard smile
Her hand covered her lips

She asked, "Do you remember when
We met at lake before?
Divergent by 200 feet,
Saw not benefactor."

"Yes, but I sent my owl to search,"
Said mage with noble mien.
"Whenever you shall call to me,
I will get to my queen."

The queen then smiled and said she knew
And patted she his cheek.
And said, "Why don't we mount your steed?
We haven't got all week!"

The queen's great beauty was renowned,
And known to everyone.
The wizard trembled at the thought
Behind him she would run.

The wizard mounted then his horse,
Extending her his hand
She settled in behind the mage
To start the ride as planned.

Beginning then the pleasant ride,
Around the fabled tow'r.
The horse broke then into a lope.
Began to feel its pow'r.

The queen then gasped and wizard knew
That something was amiss.
"My wizard dear to my fair heart,
This ride fills me with bliss.

But could we stay just at a trot?
I'm not used to such pow'r.
Your patience with me will inspire,
And confidence empow'r."

The wizard, grateful to his queen,
His fondness for her shown,
Slowed down the horse into a trot
The loping to postpone.

So rode they round the field of green
Outside the tower large
A wizard happy with his queen,
His power she would charge.

Glanced he back at royal beauty.
She smiled back at him.
Riding horse together, happy
Cup was filled to the brim.

Her eyes held his in that moment
He started there to drown.
Her long blond hair in streaming wind
And beauteous royal gown.

Conspired to solidify,
Her place within his heart.
Watched he then the path before him
Unseen smile to impart.

Soon the journey ended and he
Helped the queen to dismount.
She smiled and thanked him for the ride,
And went to her own mount.

She smiled and said that she'd had fun
And said they'd ride again.
And when she felt it comfortable
They'd ride down in the glen.

The happy wizard mounted then,
His mighty, loyal horse,
And with the monarch left the lake,
By different paths, of course.

The wizard got back to his tow'r
And became lost in thought.
He wondered how she really felt,
Did he give what she sought?

He finally concluded then
Pondering in his tow'r
He'd prob'ly give her anything
Were it within his pow'r.

THE OWL AND THE DOVE

A dove was resting in a tree,
Back from an evening glide.
She did not see the cat climb up,
And sneak up to her side.

The cat swung full and smote poor dove,
And knocked her to the ground.
All breath and sense knocked out of her,
She could not make a sound.

The cat jumped down in victory,
For he was on the prowl,
He counted his the tasty dove,
But did not count on owl.

The owl was soaring high above,
And saw the grisly scene,
And entered into bold descent,
He planned to intervene.

With silent feathers dived the owl,
As fast as he could go.
Cat bared his claws to kill and then,
Prepared the fatal blow.

The dove just closed her pretty eyes,
And waited there to die.
She did not see the hoary owl,
Descending from the sky.

But neither did the prideful cat,
Who focused on the dove,
He never saw owl's talons sharp,
That slashed him from above.

Then screeched the owl as the cat's blood,
Streamed crimson down its side,
The cat then faced impassioned owl
He would not be denied.

He said unto the snowy bird,
"You cannot the dove save,
I'll simply kill the both of you,
And send you to the grave."

The owl said, "Cat, you might do this,
Or your head I will own,
Whatever fate befalls this dove,
She'll not face it alone."

The cat said, "Owl! You can't hurt me,
But you bear many scars,
Of times we fought and you were hurt.
These bloody battles ours!"

"My beak was made to rend your flesh,
My talons like your claws,
Can cut the sinew from the bone,
And that should give you pause."

The owl continued argument,
"I can you still defy.
For you can only prowl the Earth,
And both of us can fly"

That cat said, "Logically you're right,
But still I'm mystified.
How will you soar into the blue,
When you'll not leave her side?"

The owl then mentioned to the cat,
He'd one more thing to share,
"While we engaged in our debate,
Behind you snuck the Bear!"

The cat then jumped and turned to run,
From deadly ursine threat.
A yowl of frustration let go,
As realization set.

There was no bear behind the cat,
Though one lived in the wood.
He leaped at owl to kill him there.
To catch him if he could.

In space of time made by deceit,
The owl picked up the dove,
With careful grip in talons sharp,
He winged his way above.

Tail feathers ripped from snowy bird,
They fluttered to the dirt.
He, barely missed by pouncing cat,
Disaster did avert.

He carried dove back to her nest,
And tried to use his beak.
To gently straighten feathers there,
And then she deigned to speak.

"Dear owl, I never saw the cat,
Until it was too late.
I'm grateful you would intercede,
And save me from my fate."

The owl responded, "Prowling cat,
Whom we all call Vitae,
Doesn't care who he does injure,
And makes us all his prey.

But vicious cat will never win
As long as we can fly.
For he can only prowl the Earth,
And never roam the sky.

We do have work that must be done
Way down upon the ground,
Just remember that in the skies,
Is where our homes are found."

And so the owl and lovely dove
Became the fastest friends.
She spread light and joy everywhere,
While he stopped vicious ends.

Such is the tale as it was told,
About the owl and dove,
The owl made for protection, and
The dove for peace and love.

THE DOVE AND THE OWL

The dove and owl were fastest friends,
Enjoying time to fly.
They seemed to have a special bond,
Together in the sky.

And when one day, the lovely dove
Approached the wise old bird,
With sadness in her liquid eyes
She sought to find a word.

With seeming heavy heart she said
Unto the owl at last
That she could fly with him no more
Though pleasant in the past.

She said she worried for her wings,
They seemed to hurt her so.
And but for that she'd fly with him
Above the Earth below.

The owl knew something was amiss,
He doubted pennon hurt.
For he had seen her in the sky,
On wing with other birds.

He was not sure what he did wrong,
And never would he ask.
He thought it tough enough on her
Already with this task.

Suspecting some external thing,
Had forced on her this view.
Or maybe she had just grown tired
And sought for something new.

The reasons, though, were not germane.
The end results the same.
She left to seek her happiness,
And her he could not blame.

Before she left, he mentioned that
He understood her plight.
That if she needed, he'd be there,
Even if out of sight.

He wanted her to feel no pain;
Her cup filled to the brim,
And her to have her happiness,
If even without him.

Elsewhere close by a lonely bear,
Just bowed his shaggy head,
And started for the distant peaks,
To live thereon instead.

The Wizard from his tower high,
Descended and he stood,
And looked upon the palace in
The center of the wood.

He mounted then his trusty steed,
And cantered to the East.
He left the wood on fateful quest,
To conquer loathsome beast.

The owl just took to silent wing,
And left the fading light.
Filled with the fondest memories,
He flew into the night.

THE QUEEN ON THE CLIFF

The lonely queen atop a cliff
Stood right upon the edge.
Surveying her domain below
From mountain's highest ledge.

Although her life was rich indeed,
With woodland kingdom vast.
Her royal soul seem troubled by
Decisions from the past.

To make her mind relax from court,
Some habits she had made.
She would ascend her tower in
Her palace in the glade.

She used to watch the wizard's owl
Majestic in the skies
As it soared with her lovely dove,
A wonder to her eyes.

She oft would also see the bear
So gentle for his kind.
Wait by the tree beside the brook
So pixie he could find.

She watched the pixie and the bear,
Spend time within the wood.
Developing great friendship, a
Bond both profound and good.

And then there was the wizard who
Would visit as he could.
He oft would gallop over from
His tower in the wood.

He shared his time and was her friend.
He helped her in her need.
He gave no thought to recompense.
A loyal sage indeed.

So on the cliff she stood in thought,
With wind blowing her hair,
It and white dress like pennants caught
Upon the bracing air.

Her retinue did not perceive
What action they should take.
To get their queen back from the edge,
And conversation make.

While outwardly a picture of
Her royal pow'r and grace.
A single tear escaped her eye,
And rested on her face.

The owl had not been seen in days.
He flew into the night
The dove now flew with sadness and
She missed her friend in flight.

The bear left for the mountains, and
The Pixie could not see.
A trace of her fond Ursine friend,
While waiting by their tree.

As to the queen, she'd seen the mage
Depart his place of pow'r.
She'd seen him look toward where she was,
Up in her palace tow'r.

And so he mounted trusty steed,
And headed for the plains.
She tried to stop him, but could not
Would she see him again?

Then looked she down from mountain cliff
To wizard's home below.
No lights within his tower and
From hearths no cheery glow.

She tried to mind the last thing said,
Did she the Wizard hurt?
Or by communication missed,
His loyalty divert?

Then suddenly a blast occurred.
It made a mighty sound.
The shockwave took her retinue,
And threw them to the ground.

The queen looked to the burning ground,
And saw him kneeling there.
The wizard had returned to her,
Though not in good repair.

His clothes were torn, and arms were singed;
His staff broken in two.
And crimson blood flowed from his side,
Where claw had pierced him through,

A sulfurous smoke that choked the lungs,
Spoke of the fight between.
The Wizard and the demon of
The plains of Naphthalene

He stood and limped up to the edge
Of cliff beside the queen
And in a silent moment looked
Upon the mountain scene.

He tossed his shattered staff and turned
To face his lovely queen.
And sought to kneel in deference,
To her great royal mien.

The queen took him under his arms,
And did not let him kneel.
She raised him up in an embrace,
Elation could she feel.

Her head was pressed into his chest
She felt her tears let go.
The royal tears with wizard blood,
Mixed in a heartfelt flow.

She whispered then to her found mage,
"I feared I'd lost my friend.
I've always thought that you would be
Around me to the end."

The wizard touched her queenly hair,
To show affection true.
And then looked right into her eyes,
And said, "This I tell you."

"As long as I have beating heart,
And maybe still beyond,
I will be your wizard if you
Can stand me for that long.

I thought that I'd done something wrong,
And in your favor waned,
And so I sought my demon out
Upon the horrid plain.

My thinking was that either I
Would old demon defeat,
Or I would die in battle with
My boots upon my feet.

Whichever way the battle went,
Of little consequence.
Because without your favor, my
Life is a sad pretense.

In fact the demon had me, and
Prepared the killing blow.
But then I thought I heard you cry
Upon this old plateau.

I could not bear to see you hurt,
And so my strength renewed.
I summoned all the pow'r I could
And ended mortal feud.

I gathered all the energy
From everything around
And detonated both of us
And demon did cut down.

So as the air exploded in
The hottest fire known.
I homed in on your royal tears,
And teleported home.

You have to know that never will
I leave your royal side.
No matter where I go in life,
I'll always be close by.

My power's within your command,
And you should know that if,
Your whim decided that I should,
I'd jump off of this cliff."

The queen looked up into the sky,
And saw the wizard's owl
Returned from his mysterious flight.
And then she heard a growl.

The bear, it seemed, also returned,
And waited by the tree.
He waded in the nearby brook,
'Til Pixie he would see.

She smiled at her wizard and
She said, "Welcome back home.
You must go to your tower, and
I must get to my throne.

Are you still able this to do;
Effective teleport?"
The wizard answered, "Yes, I am.
What is it you purport?"

The queen just laughed and gave a push
To wizard of the free.
And as he fell from highest cliff,
She said "You'll fall for me!"

The wizard laughed as down he fell.
She'd made a funny jest
By taking promise literally,
She put him to the test.

The queen watched laughing wizard fall
Then heard a pop of air.
Where he had just been falling down,
He was no longer there.

She stayed a couple minutes more
And thought about her pow'r.
She looked and saw some lights come up
Within the wizard's tow'r.

The queen then turned to retinue,
A smile on her face.
For everything was right again,
And all was in its place.

THE TREE AND HER OWL

In a lush and verdant meadow,
Stood a lovely tree.
She was tall and she was slender.
A great beauty she.

When the tempest around her raged
And the wind blew hard.
She would bend but not be broken
Nor be caught off guard.

For the beasts within the forest
She provided shade.
They sought shelter in her bower.
'Neath her limbs they stayed.

The tree showed love to all who came
None she turned away
Her quiet strength and boundless heart
Held the ills at bay.

One day an old owl saw her while
Finishing his hunt.
The night was done and morning sun
Owl to tree did shunt.

Soft feathers burnished in gold fire
Made the owl to glide
To her lovely upper branches
Happiness betide

The owl was happy for he found
A nice place to stay
What pleasure felt perched on her limbs
Resting there by day.

The tree was pleased to let the owl
Stay with her because.
She knew that while he nested there
She'd not feel the saws

Of lumberjacks or foresters,
The owl in plain view.
A protected species and a
Defensive purview.

The tree and owl became great friends
He made her to laugh.
With wind gently caressing bough,
Voice on her behalf.

For years the two continued on
Friends so strong and rare.
She listened to his soothing song
Show'ring him with care.

One day the owl now aged and worn
Settled on the ground,
Looked up at her as if to say,
"I've been gladly bound"

"You've been a blessing in my life."
With tears in his eyes.
He said, "I hope I blessed you too."
And beneath her died.

The tree then bent and covered him
With her petals fair.
No finer raiment ever found
The best he could wear.

The tree was sad then for some years,
Then a thought occurred
Could she still feel him perching there?
Was it spirit bird?

Could she still hear his gentle call?
Could she talons feel?
His gentle grip on favorite limbs,
Heart of tree to heal.

The tree would smile if smile she could
Never would she scowl
Forever since fast friends they were
She would keep her owl.

DIVISION VI: FELLOW SERVANTS

IN WHICH THE POET

NOTES HOW HE AND HIS

MUSE SERVE THE SAME MASTER

ARTISTRY

I am sometimes a poet, and
I think I do okay.
Words to generate emotions
And perhaps logic sway.

One evening wherein I drowsed,
In comfort on my bed.
It seemed to me I heard a voice,
Whispering in my head.

It said, "You do write pretty well.
A gift from me to you.
Creative power in your mind,
It was from me you drew.

You recognize the beauty that
I fondly put in place.
For purpose of remembering,
Your GOD's eternal grace.

As source of inspiration, then,
I'll write a poem for you.
It will be perfect, but be flawed,
This only I can do."

I thought that it might be hoot,
If I could but contrast,
This work of art from up above,
To verses from my past.

In truth I did not heed the voice.
I thought it all a dream.
Until the next day when I saw,
His work of art agleam.

The poem was full of love and grace,
A beauty to behold.
It seemed so perfect to my eyes,
Though some flaws it must hold.

I read this poem most every day,
And my low spirit flies.
For perfect poem with unseen flaws;
A woman with green eyes.

A POET'S PRAYER

O LORD, I know that thou art HE,
That gives the vision unto me.
Inspiring both the written word,
And beauty found. My spirit stirred.

I also thank thee for the gift,
Of someone to my spirit lift.
Filled both with beauty and your grace,
Inspiring me to life embrace.

A beauteous vessel, she is made
By thy great hands; no part mislaid.
Thou mad'st this blessing in my life.
To break my chains, and temper strife.

I ask thee, LORD, if it please thee,
That when my soul's required of me,
That here on Earth she will endure,
So I won't live with heartbreak sure.

And if this is some lovely dream,
My muse not real; no morning beam.
O LORD of lords before I wake,
I pray thee, LORD, my soul to take.

THE LOVER'S PRAYER

Dear LORD, please let me demonstrate
To her utmost respect
And show her that she's precious. She's
A jewel without defect.

Instill in me Thy wisdom to
Be grateful for the time
You blessed me with to spend with her
In moments most sublime.

Please grant me strength to always show
That I hold her so dear,
And nothing makes me happier
Than when she draws me near.

And if Thy will declare it so,
I ask that she might see
How much I truly cherish her,
And what she means to me.

And LORD, at last, I thank you for
Your wondrous work of art.
This woman that you put on Earth,
And also in my heart.

Edward Bowman

PALIMPSEST

The Master wished to write his words,
But found no parchment new.
So He found one written on, and
Knew that He must undo

The words that had been written there,
Both ugly and profane.
Words of human misery, and
A slave on grisly chain.

He took a tincture of his tears,
And mixed it with his blood.
Applied it to the parchment and,
The old ink turned to mud.

With loving hands He made it clean.
The parchment fresh and white.
And then in ink that will not fade,
Began His words to write.

This vellum scroll on which he wrote,
I hope that you can see,
Is really just a metaphor.
The palimpsest is me.

He still looks for old parchment that
He can remake as new
Will he find in your darkest hour
A palimpsest in you?

SALVATION

Many years ago I chose to
Serve almighty GOD,
Partaking in salvation free
To humankind so flawed.

Since then my life has been quite good,
Although I still have pain.
For mankind needs its tests to grow
And higher place attain.

One issue that ofttimes occurs,
When life becomes a grind,
We start to live as if by rote,
And joy has left our mind.

With life like this, we soon forget
The colors and the sounds,
And beauty made by breath of GOD
Which all of us surrounds.

And sometimes at a bleakest hour,
When all your light is dim,
HE sends you someone to remind
How blessed you are by HIM.

This happened just last year to me.
She burst upon the scene.
Wreathed in exquisite beauty, and
The grace fit for a queen.

Although these things are pleasing, true,
They're not the greatest part
Her inner light and kindness fueled
By GOD sets her apart.

So, when she deigned to be my friend
And spend some of her time
She pushed me back out of my rut,
From which I could not climb.

My life now full of sights and sounds,
With beauty all around.
I see all I had forgotten.
My mind has been unbound.

I'm not sure what would happen if
She ever went away.
I wonder if my life would change
Back to its shades of gray.

GOD saved me from my certain death,
Which threatened like a knife.
Then HE sent her to befriend me,
And save me from my life.

SEEKING MAN

I saw a fold of lovely sheep.
Their number ninety-nine.
The Shepherd seemed so resolute,
"The lost one I must find".

The fold secured, he left to find
The one that went away,
To wander in the wilderness
Where wolves are seeking prey.

The Shepherd searched both high and low.
Then bleating did he hear.
In a ravine beset by wolves
He found sheep filled with fear.

The Shepherd ran down to the sheep,
And mighty wolves did smite.
He gathered up the wounded sheep,
And saved it from its plight.

He took the sheep back to the fold,
And made all to rejoice.
The sheep then never wandered far
From sound of Master's voice.

This is a story we all know,
But there is something deep.
Something that we ought to embrace,
And in our mem'ry keep.

You see, there is a difference vast
With The Almighty's plan.
While men are seeking their false gods,
The true GOD's seeking man.

THE ANGEL'S REVELATION

I see the angel that sees her,
And sought with him to speak.
I asked about his lovely ward,
This woman so unique.
Upon me did he fix his gaze,
I fell down overawed.
He bade me rise and said that we
Both serve the living GOD.

He put his hand against my head,
I felt my mind give way.
I heard him say, "I'll show you truth,
about her yet today."
In one breath's span we traveled back,
In time, but not abroad.
And saw a younger version of
This woman made by GOD.

I looked upon her from above.
She seemed as if she glowed.
She was with child and her delight,
In stately visage showed.
I heard an infant's beating heart.
This lovely sound I laud.
It beat mere inches from her own,
A precious gift from GOD.

We traveled then two years ahead.
She'd had a baby girl
Who I saw cradled in her arms,
Protected from this world.
The daughter looked in mother's eyes,
And saw there no facade,
But saw the truest love on Earth.
Just like the love of GOD.

The angel took me by the arm,
and leapt some years ahead.
The daughter suffered fever and
she languished on her bed.
The mother moved the Earth and heav'n
The illness to defraud,
And to her fevered daughter showed,
A love most like our GOD's

The angel showed a thousand points
Of moments throughout time.
Where she great love her daughter showed;
A mother's love sublime.
He said, "The way she lives her life
With perfect love unflawed,
Has made her daughter come to know,
The profound love of GOD."

The angel took me far beyond
the time I left this Earth,
to when her days were now complete,
And she'd see heaven's worth.
I saw the gentle shadows close
around her with the sod,
I wept for her although I knew
That she is loved by GOD.

He said, "These should be tears of joy,
Although she there lays low.
This is when you'll see her again,
In time's natural flow.
But take note of these myriad points
Of light where quickened trod.
Each one a person who by her,
Now know the love of GOD."

The angel took me back to where
we first began to speak.
I saw her full of life again.
A tear slid down my cheek.
He said, "You need to cherish her.
I know you need no prod.
For everywhere this woman goes,
She shows the love of GOD."

THE CONFLICT

I have an inner conflict, though
This really isn't new.
This happens to each of the saints,
Because of natures two.

On one hand we are human, and
We enter into sin.
The other nature Christian, which
Defines our light within.

Is something wrong with happiness,
That it must be denied?
That some decisions made in youth,
Make life with pain supplied?

This is the root of the conflict;
To do what is deemed right
When human nature tells you that
You do not want to fight.

When there is someone or something
That brings you happiness,
It's human to seek after them,
And mitigate distress.

And then it might be only once
Per lifetime so finite,
That someone perfect comes along,
A bright and glorious light.

The conflict comes when someone else,
Should be providing light.
Our human part seeks for a source,
To end eternal night.

The Christian nature less concerned
With feelings borne within,
Than answering the question, "Is
This action filled with sin?"

I'm glad that we are under grace,
'Cause there's no end in sight
To conflicts, but this current one,
I do not wish to fight.

THE HAMMER

I saw a cross atop a hill,
With setting sun behind.
The soldiers at the base of it
To prisoner assigned.

The prisoner was hanging there.
Nailed to the ugly cross.
I looked and I was overcome
With dreadful sense of loss.

As I ran up to render aid,
A soldier took a spear.
And thrust it deep into his side
While other soldiers jeered.

His blood and water mingled there,
And flowed down holy side.
It seemed to flow throughout the world.
A river deep and wide.

I turned to face the people that
Were gathered at his feet.
Confronting both the soldiers and
Civilians on the street.

Demanding, "Who's responsible
For killing righteous man?"
'Twas then I saw the hammer that
I held within my hand.

THE RAINBOW

She huddled down against the storm.
The driving rain did not feel warm.
The lightning struck. The tempest howled.
The blackened clouds upon her scowled.

It seemed like hours that it rained.
The downpour on her unrestrained.
She prayed to GOD the rain should cease.
That by HIS will the storm decrease.

What then beheld she with her eyes?
The storm clouds yielding to blue skies.
The storm had ceased and up on high,
A rainbow formed up in the sky.

She then remembered how it formed.
Water in air the light transformed.
Multiple colors cross the sky,
A grateful tear starts in her eye.

She knew import lied not in how,
But why the rainbow showed up now.
Reminder of promise to man
To never flood whole Earth again.

In whispered prayer she thanked the Lord,
For promise kept; ancient concord.
Saw she then a light that beckoned.
Beyond reach as mankind reckoned.

The light was from the living God,
The brilliance of it overawed.
Majestic colors put to shame
Beauteous rainbow of ancient fame.

Towards the light, she briskly travelled,
Wanting mystery unraveled.
Soon she stood as close as she could,
Basked in the light of all that's good.

Coalescing light then furnished
Cross with blood and tears both burnished.
This wondrous cross, the only kind.
Providing light to all mankind.

She turned her eyes up to the skies.
The light of God within her eyes.
She cried and bowed her lovely face,
And felt the power of His grace.

So on this cross we made of wood
A savior died where sinners should
New covenant sealed by His name,
By which mankind escapes the flame.

THE SACRIFICE

She looked into the mirror,
And liked not what she saw,
A black smudge on the softest skin,
A human's fatal flaw.

Trying she to clean the smudge
She wiped at the black stain.
The smudge just grew to larger size
The ugly mark of Cain.

She looked down at her right hand
The tar was there as well
The more she tried to clean it off,
The more it stained her shell.

Started then, the tears to fall,
The smudge was like gangrene.
She could not stop its ugly spread
Herself she could not clean.

She ran to the doctor's house,
She could not stop the tears.
She did not like the filth on her,
One of her greatest fears.

Physician looked at patient
And said he knew the cure
The cost of it was very high,
But it would make her pure.

She asked what the cure entailed,
How would she be made clean?
The doctor said he would explain,
Before the cure was seen.

The doctor had a good Son.
Who had a blood type rare,
His blood could cure ugly disease,
All damage, too, repair.

She said she needed rare cure
With stain she could not live.
She asked how much would be the cost.
Counting what she could give.

The doctor mentioned to her,
The cost had all been paid
All he needed was her consent
And he'd heal her today.

She looked at her filthy stain,
And started then to weep.
She knew she needed to be healed,
From blot that ran so deep.

In hand the doctor took her,
And led her to the back.
Where there she saw a red tinged pool
Beneath a graven plaque.

The plaque was dedicated to
The memory of the Son.
The cure had taken all his blood
A victory hard won.

Sadly then she entered in,
Submerging in the pool.
And rose to walk refreshed in life
The doc pulled up his stool.

He tested for any smudge,
That still might have remained
He said she was completely healed,
And would remain unstained.

He said the cure had cost much
For it, his Son had died.
But all he asked for her to do,
Was the cure not to hide.

She went back into her house,
And stood before the mirror.
Clothed in beauty now made perfect,
By spirit that is clear.

Overjoyed, she went through life,
Defined by wondrous grace,
Her beauty most men wondered at,
But source they could not place.

Then one day she met a man
Who became dearest friend.
He knew about the doctor's cure,
Of beauty from within.

He spent some time around her,
He a devoted one.
He thanked the doctor every day,
For cure powered by Son.

Sacrifice had cured her ill,
And cleansed his stain as well.
In full health under Doctor's care,
The two of them would dwell.

Of course, the sacrifice was,
Not just for two alone,
The great Son's blood was given for
The whole world to atone.

THE VESSELS

Once there were two vessels,
Both by The Potter made
One was strong but non descript
The other with beauty staid.

Both were filled with water,
Pure from the Potter's source.
They both fulfilled their function
As a matter of due course.

The stout one saw slender,
And felt a rush of joy
Put on the shelf together
Their perfection to enjoy.

Was one in strength perfect?
Though scars and scratches borne?
Was the other in beauty
True perfection to adorn?

Potter looked upon them
With loving smile he told,
"You both are strong and also
Beautiful, each in your mold.

Both great beauty and great strength
Is not in outward spin,
But perfection is attained
By the Water held within."

Edward Bowman

DIVISION VII: EPILOGUE

IN WHICH THE POET

FINISHES HIS WORK

AND BRIEFLY PUTS ASIDE

HIS PEN TO BE

INSPIRED ANOTHER DAY

THE HEART ATTACK

I finally had a heart attack.
My genes and lifestyle paid me back.
As doctors worked on failing heart,
I could not help but thinking start.

I catalogued any regret
I had in case my sun had set.
I thought I might regret surmise,
For having little exercise,

Or eating poorly for my health,
My heart disease was not by stealth!
I found that I cared not at all,
About my lifestyle and downfall.

I hoped without regret to die,
And make clean journey to the sky.
For eating right and exercise,
Does not stop truth: everyone dies.

For me, my death I do not fear,
I would not shed a single tear.
For I lived well, and by a plan,
And kindness showed to fellow man.

Alas, this made me think of her,
And also my emotions stir.
And so I found my one regret,
I felt my eyes becoming wet.

How would she feel if I should die,
Without her saying a goodbye?
And maybe would she want to be,
An angel sent to comfort me.

Or maybe she could not come by,
To sit with me and watch me die.
I think it could be hard on her,
Should GOD my soul to HIM transfer.

I found regret and wished that I,
Had one more chance before I died.
To see her face and hold her hand
And ask her from a dying man

For her forgiveness for my part,
If ever I wounded her heart.
And did she know I held her dear?
Or had I never made this clear?

And so it was I closed my eyes,
With heartache I could not disguise.
I hoped that she would be OK,
And come to visit me some day.

LIFELINE

It was not very long ago,
Because I let it slide,
My health was in a dismal state,
And finally I died.

My consciousness just slipped away.
My spirit drifted up.
I saw my body lying there,
The ultimate breakup.

I saw the thinnest silver cord,
Attached to spirit chest.
Trace down to the most silent clay;
My body at its rest.

'Twas at this point I thought of her,
And realized then with fear,
That I'd not see her for some time,
And could not her be near.

I saw the faintest silver cord
Just slightly thicker grow,
And felt the rise of my poor soul
Abruptly start to slow.

My spirit shed a crystal tear
As I then brought to mind,
The fondest mem'ries of my life.
Which I might leave behind.

The cord was thick and growing now.
Pulling my spirit down.
Towards my still body on the bed
Swathed in a standard gown.

So then, at last, I brought to mind
The image of her face.
Remembering her inner light,
And how she's clothed with grace.

I saw her eyes that showed to me
The beauty of her soul.
The silver cord then snapped me back,
And once more made me whole.

I felt her hand pressed into mine
And opened up my eyes.
I saw her sitting next to me
Attending my demise.

She cried to see me laid so low,
I touched her tear stained cheek,
And silent tears slid from my eyes
As she began to speak.

I closed my eyes and listened well,
But not just to the words.
Her dulcet tones washed over me,
And life within me stirred.

She mention to me heartfelt things.
Expressing deepest bond.
That she preferred me not to die,
And go to the beyond.

I looked into her soulful eyes,
And gently touched her hair.
Emotions in a tumult raged,
Their depth beyond compare.

I told her that I'd do my best
To postpone heaven's call,
But that this final debt in life
Is one that's owed by all.

Continuing to hold her hand -
It was so soft in mine -
I closed my eyes to take my rest
And thought of a lifeline.

Just like a sailor overboard,
And line thrown from a ship,
To which he'll cling to be pulled back
Held in a vice like grip.

I wondered if she realized
That she would always give
A lifeline that might pull me back;
A reason I should live.

DYING TO GET THERE

Once, when I was still on the Earth
I knew a woman fair.
Beautiful even as she was
That's not what made me care.
She had this inner light that shone,
'Twas bright for all to see
She was filled up with grace and love,
And captivated me,
It seemed that wherever she was,
I really didn't care,
But had the thought run through my mind,
"I'm dying to get there."

Together, we ofttimes would walk
Upon a country trail
We would converse and share some laughs,
We'd spin some epic tales.
Not long after we started this,
It was special to me.
I loved to spend my time with her;
A special woman she.
She had much to divide her time,
Her duties gladly bear
So when she'd ask to with me walk,
"I'm dying to get there!"

Sometimes we'd go to the ballpark.
It was my favorite place.
The fans and sights, and sounds, and smells,
Brought smiles to my face.
But what made these trips seem complete,
How perfect days were made.
Was just because she was there too.
Whether she watched or played.
So, since this was my favorite place,
Found the Summer glare,
When we would go to see a game,
"I'm dying to get there!"

At other times, we both would ride
On horses made of steel.
The rush of wind through long blond hair,
True freedom we could feel.
With destination not in mind,
Just riding for the thrill,
We felt our stress just melt away,
And bonded closer still.
So when she ever asked of me,
A ride with her to share,
I simply asked just when and where,
"I'm dying to get there."

So, over years our friendship grew.
Inseparable the bond.
Amazing times with someone who,
Engendered feelings fond.
Whether we'd go to catch a flick,
Or boat upon a lake,
Or dine at various restaurants,
Our own fun we would make.
Whatever thing we chose to do,
And, too, no matter where,
My heart did flips within my chest,
"I'm dying to get there!"

It is appointed once for man,
To pay the final debt.
With no exception made for me,
I died without regret.
She held my hand with silent tears,
To share my final breath.
She was the last thing my eyes saw,
Before they closed in death.
I told her, "I am dying well,
Now please do not despair
Heaven's my next adventure, and
I'm dying to get there."

THE REAPER

I sat in my friend's hospice room,
His time was almost up.
Our other friends gathered as well.
To help him drink death's cup.

I heard a knock upon the door,
And got up from my chair.
I motioned everyone to sit,
For visitor I'd care

I opened up the room's wide door,
To admit knocking friend.
Saw skinless face in ebon robe,
Herald of colleague's end.

Crestfallen did I back away,
To let him in the door.
Futility to try to stop
His necessary chore.

I backed away to give him room,
And turned back to my chair.
Cold sweat broke out when I first saw
My body still was there.

I turned, aghast, to face my fate,
I thought, "This can't be true."
In voice sepulchral, reaper said,
"The bell now tolls for you"

Instinctively, I backed away,
Though unafraid to die.
I scanned the room for blond haired friend,
And tried to catch her eye.

She turned as if she thought she saw,
A flicker with her eye,
I only wanted one last hug,
To tell my friend goodbye.

She gently frowned as if she knew
That something had transpired.
Though realized not that she had lost
The man whom she inspired.

I turned to face the reapers form,
And made a mournful plea,
"Please let me say goodbye to her,
Before my soul's set free."

The reaper said, "This cannot be,
Your time on Earth is passed.
Ordained this is for everyone;
Unsaid things at the last.

Seeing the fondness you both shared,
And level of her faith,
Perceive do I she'll visit you,
And see her friend the wraith."

The reaper then changed up his form;
A being bathed in light.
An angel come to escort me
To realms beyond the night.

And so I went into my grave,
And waited there to see,
The time when my beloved friend
Would come and visit me.

THE WRAITH REMEMBERED

I saw you come to visit me.
It was a nice surprise!
As beautiful as ever, though,
I saw you not with eyes.

For now I see in spectrums that
The human eye cannot.
I can see now what once was veiled
Your beauty heaven wrought.

I saw some tears spill down your cheek,
you whispered 'neath your breath.
That still you missed me every day,
And had so since my death.

Some comfort then, I tried to give;
I tried to hold your hand.
But ghostly grasp through quickened flesh,
Slipped through as if 'twere banned.

I think you might have noticed me.
You gave a little start.
Your widened eyes, the little gasp,
And palm pressed to your heart.

And then I saw you shake your head,
You knew it could not be.
The ghost of your dear friend in life,
The restless wraith of me.

Then I became compassionate,
And gently touched your hair
It seems I made the wind whip up,
And blow it everywhere.

You smiled then, e'en through your tears,
And put the flowers down.
You touched the stone above my head,
And over me knelt down.

"I don't know if it's really you",
You said with tearing eyes.
"Because you always made me smile,
I would not be surprised".

You patted then the granite stone
And said you'd come again.
I hope it isn't hard on you,
I don't want you in pain.

And then I saw you turn to go.
I started then to cry.
The ghostly tears on specter's face
Became rain from the sky.

You looked through rain that strangely fell.
From cloudless sky above,
Then smiled and pointed to my grave.
A smile filled with love.

After you left, I sat on stone.
Began to reminisce
Of us in life, and pleasant times,
And all that I now miss.

I know that I will see you soon,
though I'm outside of time.
I hope you know I'll miss you, though,
The rest of your lifetime.

When comes the day you are summ'd,
To tend the LORD as well.
I hope that he will give me leave
To show you where you'll dwell.

I think we'll laugh and maybe cry
And share a quick embrace.
I'll tell you all this story, as
We go to heaven's place.

NAMES

The morning beam guides sojourner.
The owl soars with the dove.
He also roosts in slender tree,
In branches up above.

The Pixie and the Bear are friends.
They dwell within the wood.
With woman on the pedestal,
And man who understood.

The pretty Winter flower, and
Her scholar in the field,
Are close to man stabbed through the heart,
And she who his heart healed.

A friendly wraith who haunts his grave,
And she who heeds unseen.
Are watched by loyal wizard and
His beautiful, kind queen.

Two vessels on the Master's shelf
Sitting there side by side,
Contrast with addict and his drug,
Which makes his spirit glide.

Inspired by his lovely muse,
The poet writes his verse.
While man and woman live nearby
A chasm with a curse.

A funny software engineer
Who fell into the skies.
And lovely Christian woman with
Her captivating eyes.

THE PIRATE QUEEN

I watched the Pirate Queen depart
She seemed to me a piece of art.
Her beauty is beyond belief,
The hearts she steals feel great relief.

She walked upon the wooden pier,
Her salty crew let out a cheer.
For they loved going out to sea,
Where she rules them, but they feel free.

In leathers clad with long soft hair,
She smelled the salty seaside air.
And boarded she her fearsome ship
Preparing soon to leave the slip.

But what was this? She looked at me!
I wondered, could this truly be?
For though I'd known her for some time,
I work with all the dockside grime.

A lowly dockhand labored I,
Could one like me catch a queen's eye?
'Twas then I saw her at me smile,
I felt the warmth and basked a while.

Then, suddenly, with movement fast,
She reached into her waistband sash,
And threw a knife toward my head,
I had not thought she'd want me dead!

The knife was buried in the wood,
Of the dock pylon where I stood.
She laughed and then she pointed there,
Then turned and left without a care.

I watched her sail out to the sea,
This pirate queen of great beauty.
Once her great ship was lost to sight,
I saw her knife in the sunlight.

I found that it contained a note,
Which I opened and read by rote.
I read it and my heart did swell,
I wiped my eyes for they did well.

Surprised I was to find that she,
Had entertained some thought for me.
That night before I went to bed,
I thought of what the note had said.

"My dearest dockhand know that I
Will every night look in the sky.
And there will find the northern star,
Which you can see from where you are.

And when you look at it at night,
I'll also put it in my sight.
So that no matter where I go
You'll be with me in star's soft glow."

Now every night I go outside
And let the North star be my guide.
I climb a hill and find the star
That joins me with the queen afar.

I feel my heart fill up with care,
For I can feel her presence there.
I'll do this while she is at sea,
Until the queen returns to me.

CARIBBEAN PERFECTION

Outside she lays upon her bed.
A pillow soft beneath her head.
With tropic sun high in the skies,
Reflected in her liquid eyes,

She never fails to me amaze,
And holds me in her loving gaze.
My pulse is quickened. I can't leave.
I find that I no longer breathe.

She seems to call me with her eyes,
To balcony on which she lies.
Her ruby lips and soft blond hair;
Her perfumed scent upon the air,

Conspire to draw me close to her,
And make something within me stir.
Is this a dream? She's next to me.
In perfect femininity.

Her eyes seem like two verdant gems,
Two perfect crystals draw me in.
Someone this perfect comes along,
But once within a lifetime long.

I sometimes wonder what she spies
With her two glorious emerald eyes.
Does she see in me caring man
Who will be there for a life span?

My soul is bared. Defense is gone.
My spirit sings conflicted song.
On one hand she is dear to me;
This princess of the Southern Sea.

Yet circumstance and fate conspire.
Restraining that which is desired,
And just like guiding northern star,
I must her cherish from afar.

Edward Bowman

READY FOR BED

The perfect woman ends her day,
And readies for her bed.
She brushes through her soft blond hair,
Which, lovely, crowns her head.

She then applies some lotion to
Her tan and supple skin.
Then has a last look in the mirror,
And smiles at girl therein.

Her night gown is of finest silk
The hem down to mid thigh.
The cloth caresses her soft skin,
She gives contented sigh.

She moves to stand beside the bed,
The covers she draws back.
She gently slides between the sheets,
And lays upon her back.

Her pillow blessed to hold her head,
The rest by bed embraced.
The room, though darkened, still reveals
This bed by beauty graced.

She stretches most luxuriously,
And changes how she lies.
Now that she is so comfortable,
She slowly shuts her eyes.

In her mind's eye she sees the stress
Encountered through the day,
As bubbles in a placid lake
Rising to go away.

The bubbles rise up to the top,
And dissipate in air.
She smiles and she sighs once more.
Her mind drifts now elsewhere.

As breathing slows she starts to fade,
She thinks of one last thing.
Her smile slightly grows and then,
Sublime sleep brings sweet dreams.

I am given to wonder what
Was the last thing she thought.
Before descending into dreams
With love and beauty fraught.

It might have been a river that
Flows to a distant sea.
With barges in the dusk that sail
On river silently.

Perhaps it was a hoary owl,
That flew on silent wing.
A guardian protecting her
Whilst in a pleasant dream.

Perchance it was a memory,
Of someone from the past,
Or maybe just a feeling that
Sweet sleep was here at last.

No matter what it was she thought,
Or content of her dream.
The scene is very beautiful.
The sleeping morning beam.

THE FOURTH WALL

He stood atop a mountain peak,
And struck a hero's pose.
His hair whipped by the freshest wind,
Which also tugged his clothes.

He looked down to the plain below,
And saw great beauty there.
The beauty made him think of her,
And touching soft blonde hair.

As if his thoughts had summoned her,
Up mountain path she came.
He could not help but smile at her,
And beckon her by name.

As she got close, he noticed that
She seemed a little sad.
He asked that she disclose to him,
What had her feeling bad.

A moment passed. She did not speak,
But put her hand in his.
She turned to him with tear in eye,
"I must tell you what is.

You are not real, and neither is
The mountain where we stand.
You're both a figment of his mind.
Made by a poet's hand."

He laughed and said, "I do not know,
What kind of jest you make.
But feel my arm, and touch my face.
Do you think I feel fake?

Or smell the heather at our feet,
And face into the wind.
Perfect sensations all around,
With you, my beauteous friend."

She said, "I know it seems that way.
With everything aligned.
But this detailed perfection is
The power of his mind."

He answered her, "I cannot think
That this world isn't true.
For if I am not truly here,
Then neither, dear, are you"

She said, "But no. I am quite real,
And never will despise,
To see how beautiful I look
When seeing through his eyes."

The man just took a moment to
Digest all that was said.
He finally laughed and said that all
This thinking hurt his head.

She stamped her pretty foot at him,
And said, "I will this prove!
There are some rules we cannot break,
For he would disapprove.

For instance, early in this poem
You beckoned me by name.
I challenge you to bellow it
So all can hear the same."

He said, "You're talking crazy, for
You know your name I know."
She said, "But you can't say it, for
Good reason even so.

You see, although most poems he writes,
Are written just for me,
He needs for other readers to
Their own woman here see."

He said, "This is not any proof.
I clearly know your name.
I think that you are poking fun,
Though I don't know the game."

"Yet still you have not said it and,
Again, you never will.
For this rule is unbreakable,
And is unbroken still.

But here is something else I'll show,
To make you soon believe.
I'll need for you to back away.
For he'll make you stop me."

"I do not wish to back away.
I like you by my side.
And pleasant is your hand in mine.
No. Here I will abide."

She screamed and pointed, "WHAT IS THAT!!??"
He turned to face a foe.
And while he was thus occupied,
She thirty feet did go.

He turned and saw her with a knife,
And asked her, "Why the ruse?"
She said, "I have to show you that
I really am his muse.

You see another stricture laid
Within the poet's mind.
Is that I cannot come to harm
Within this world designed."

He realized then what she would do,
And begged her please to stop.
He could not bear to see her death
Upon the mountain top.

"But what if you are wrong, my dear?
Please put down ugly knife.
If you should take yourself from me,
What shall I do with life?"

She smiled at him and held his eyes,
As she began her stroke.
She moved to stab into her neck,
And my resolve she broke.

I quickly changed the knife into
A snorkel in her hand.
And then I saw the shock-ed look,
Upon created man.

As rubber mouthpiece hit her neck,
And made a sound like, "Flob"
I laughed that she had played me well,
And now I had a job

With laughing sigh I entered in,
The strangest poem I wrote.
And stood upon the mountaintop
Wreathed both in flame and smoke.

I wondered why I was on fire
And realized that they'd see
Me as some sort of frightful god,
Though it was only me.

The man had fainted straight away,
And so I let him lie
I turned and looked upon her there,
She seemed about to cry.

I sent the flames and smoke away,
And bid her to come near.
I said, "Well played, now please tell me
Just why you want me here."

She said, "I wanted just to see,
The man who wrote the poems.
In gratefulness to thank him for
These homes away from home."

Then drew she near and sought to put,
Her hand upon my cheek.
I cautioned her to stop right there,
"This isn't for the weak."

But she was brave and did she try,
To touch me with her hand.
Her hand just passed through solid flesh,
'Twas something she'd not planned.

The realization hit her face,
That she, too, wasn't real.
She slumped down to the rocky ground,
Not sure what she should feel.

Although she tried, she could not stop
The flow of crystal tears
She looked at me with liquid eyes
And shared with me her fears.

She said, "I am filled with such fear,
About what will occur
When you decide the poem should end,
My life is yours, great sir."

I said, "You're looking at it wrong,
Because you do not see.
That being here within a poem,
Grants immortality.

As long as someone reads this poem,
You'll always be alive,
And get to meet me once again,
And learn for what you strive.

You see, this is not the first time,
I came to visit you,
Nor will it ever be the last,
As long as readers view."

I bore her up and sent her down,
The rocky mountain path,
And made the man that was with her,
Forget what came to pass.

I had her live 100 years.
Her beauty did not fade.
She lived her life in happiness,
Due to the gift I gave.

She knew she was immortal and
Could never really die.
Sometimes I saw her look for me,
While looking toward the sky.

So when I thought the poem should end,
I gently let her pass,
and went back to attend to her,
And laid her on the grass.

Some purple flowers lovely strewn
About her on the ground.
I made this place filled with such light
All beauty did surround.

A marker placed I by her head,
Upon it was inscribed
The 18th Sonnet by Shakespeare,
Because what it described.

Before I left I made it so
Everything would be kept
Frozen like this without decay.
I knelt by her and wept.

Returned did I unto our world,
And dried my welling eyes.
She always will be happy there,
Although I did disguise

As beautiful as I made her,
She never could compare
To the real woman that inspired,
And filled my heart with care.

HOW BEAUTIFUL THE SEASONS

In Spring when flowers lovely bloom,
And all of nature wakes
to live resplendently again,
And Winter's hold it shakes,
I notice beauty all around,
and see it genuflect.
In deference to beauty true.
In her is no defect.

Then Summer comes with blazing heat,
Its rays more beauty show.
Surrounded in the light and warmth
We bask within the glow.
Yet even with the beauty there,
That bids our passions rise.
It does not stir me half as much
As looking in her eyes.

When Fall arrives and nature starts
Preparing for its sleep
In oranges, reds and earthy hues,
Its beauty does it keep.
As leaves fall to the cooling ground;
A lovely Autumn scene.
It pales before a woman with
The bearing of a queen

As Winter blankets everything
In cold and snow alike,
Though frigid, it still beauty has;
Both pristine and ghostlike.
While nature hibernates beneath
The purest blanket made,
I see the Winter, beautiful,
Endorse her beauty staid.

And thus we see that beauty true,
The seasons all transcend
This woman makes her place within
The minds and hearts of men,
I wish that I had better skill
With which I could impart,
The grace with which she walks through life,
And place within my heart.

SHEATHING THE PEN

I finished a commissioned work,
And let my pen take rest.
I took some time to read the poems
And my own art digest.

But are they really just my own?
Or owned by all who read?
Or by the muse I wrote them for?
A lovely muse indeed.

We all have heard how mighty is
The Pen compared to Sword
For one converts by violence,
The other by the word.

So words can work to change one's mind
And let one beauty see.
Or warn about the darker side
Of frail humanity.

The sword can only rule by fear,
And sometimes will protect.
But without changing people's minds,
There's no lasting effect.

With words given with love and truth,
And crafted with some skill,
The world can see what's beautiful,
And we can live fulfilled.

But like a sword, words are just tools,
Within a human's hands.
They can be used for hate and lies,
And make ugly demands.

My purpose when I use my pen?
To always show my love
For life and for my fellow man,
And for the LORD above.

So, even with the darker poems
They're meant only to show
The effects we might bear for our
Decisions made below.

But, like a sword, the mighty pen
Must finally be sheathed.
To let all that will read the words,
Discover what's bequeathed.

A century of poems is reached.
It seems a fitting end.
Until I pick it up anon,
I sheathe the mighty pen.

ABOUT THE AUTHOR

Edward Bowman grew up in the St. Louis metropolitan area on the Illinois side of the river. He has always had an interest in the arts. In addition to writing, he also enjoys music and painting. He met his Muse in Indiana while on assignment writing documentation for software for a development house. He and Aurora keep in touch and see each other when they can. He still lives by the mighty Mississippi, in Missouri, on his small farm with his horse and four dogs.

ABOUT THE MUSE

Aurora Dawn was born and raised on Cayman Brac in the Caribbean. Since her family could trace their lineage back to royalty, and her name lent itself to such interpretation, she lightheartedly became known as "Princess" to friends and family. She traveled extensively for the software company she represented, and always seemed to leave people happier than she found them. She met Edward in Indiana when the company needed her there for an upcoming release. After finishing this assignment, she returned to her Caribbean home via cruise ship. She lives in a house by the beach with her cat, Biscuit.